POINTS OF VIEW

POINTS of VIEW

A collection of letters written to the popular BBC 1 television programme

Selected, Edited and Commented on
by
BARRY TOOK

British Broadcasting Corporation

This book is dedicated to the thousands of people who have written to me on the subject of television and without whom, all too obviously, the programme would not have been possible.

Wherever possible, permission to reprint viewers' letters has been sought and given by the individuals concerned, and I would like to thank them all for their cooperation. Where the correspondent has not supplied their address or where we've been unable to trace them, I hope and trust they will not object to the inclusion of their letter in this compilation.

Published by the
British Broadcasting Corporation
35 Marylebone High Street
London W1M 4AA

ISBN 0 563 17953 8

First published 1981

Printed in England by
The Pitman Press, Bath

Contents

Introduction

Points Of View first saw the light of day on 2 October 1961. It flourished in the capable hands of Robert Robinson until September 1965.

Kenneth Robinson took over in October 1965 and held the fort nobly until August 1967. In '68 the programme returned, again with Robert Robinson in the chair, until 26 September 1971 when, for the time being, *Points Of View* disappeared from the screen.

The Robinsons (no relation) weren't the only presenters. The archives show that many well-known names made fleeting appearances. In 1962 there were Alan Brien, Frank Weir and Alan Melville; in 1963 Trevor Lucas; in 1964 Beryl Cook, Steve Race, and Peter Bull; in 1965 Henry Fairlie, Philip Oakes, Harold Lang, and David Rees; and in 1969, '70 and '71 the records show one appearance in each year from Alan Bennett.

There have been other programmes expressing viewers' attitudes. *Nationwide* has tackled the subject in a variety of forms, and from 1967 until 1972 a TV programme called *Talk Back* flourished, in which viewers could confront producers and heads of departments (typically on 1 November 1972 the two men in the hot seat were Bill Cotton and Jonathan Miller, plus a guest appearance from Johnny Speight), and there was also a series called *Write On* which tackled viewers' gripes on a wider range of subjects but which always included at least one 'beef' about TV. But *Points Of View* itself hibernated.

Then in 1979, Bill Cotton, now Deputy Managing Director of BBC Television but then Controller of BBC 1, bought a number of American comedies and planned to show them in the 10.30 to 11 pm spot in London and the South-East on Friday evenings. Now, the trouble with American half-hour comedies is that they only last 25 minutes, the balance being taken up by commercials, and it was suggested that to fill up the odd five minutes preceding *Bilko* or *I Love Lucy, Points Of View* could be revived. It was agreed. The producer, Colin Ward-Lewis, asked me to present it, it was trailed, that is to say people were asked to write to the reborn programme, and on 31 August 1979 at 10.30 pm, *Points Of View* was back on the air.

After the opening titles, a clever sequence where my head appeared to revolve on a postage stamp – and which was lampooned subsequently by Griff Rhys Jones in *Not The Nine O'Clock News* – I said 'Hello, and welcome to a new series of the programme that airs your view about BBC television. Judging by most of the letters we've received so far viewers feel they've been having a raw deal lately.' And away we went.

The programme quickly built an enthusiastic audience in the London area and in February 1980 it was decided that a) it should now be ten minutes long, b) it would be transmitted at 8.50 on Friday evenings, c) it would be shown nationally. And, apart from weeks off at Christmas, Easter and a summer break, we've been at it ever since.

On the first programme the letter readers were Michael McClain and Janie Booth, on the second Michael was joined by John Leeson and Angela Piper (yes, she's Jennifer in the Archers). Other readers have included Astley Jones, Anna Barry, and Joanna Palmer, but the mainstays of the programme in 79/80 were Michael McClain, Angela Piper, Marie Sutherland, and Alec Bregonzi. For the 1981 season, Anna Barry and Cass Allen joined McClain and Bregonzi as the regular letter readers. In the summer of 1980, Colin Ward-Lewis was involved in other projects and the production chores were taken over, very ably, by Tim Simmons, and his assistant, Cathie Frazer. In the first months of *Points Of View* we received an average of forty letters a week. Today we receive on average a thousand letters a week. All are read, sorted, re-read, and I write a script based on the letters that seem to me to represent what people are feeling during that particular week. People are uninhibited in expressing their views and I personally find the exercise most stimulating.

There is one curious phenomenon I'd like to comment on here; it's what I describe as 'the tidal effect'. If we quote critical views of a television programme it can be guaranteed that the next week we'll receive a shoal of letters in praise of the show and *vice versa*. I never have to provide 'balance'. Our correspondents do that for me.

Why do people write to *Points Of View*?

On the face of it merely to express an opinion about BBC programmes, but actually I believe there's a lot more to it than that. Some people just like to hear their names read out, although a surprising number ask not to have their names mentioned. Others like to share a joke or a witticism, others write just to let off steam, and in the vast majority of cases the very act of writing the letter releases the pent-up anger. Most correspondents know that their letter only has a slim chance of getting onto the screen, and regular viewers know that often only a part of the letter will be read, but people write in hope as well as in rage and we try to express as many different viewpoints as possible.

At the receiving end, the producer and I try to do two things; the first is to make sure that we select a representative sample of the week's views, the second is to find the letters that best express the opinions of the group. I've never felt it sufficient to use letters that say merely 'I like *Blake's Seven*' or 'I hate *Dallas*', but there are always a number (more than we can ever use) of letters so full of insight, delight, rage, humour (both conscious and unconscious) and well-thought-out criticism that it is never difficult to put a programme together that expresses those well-shaped views.

I am, from time to time, accused of flippancy and a general lack of seriousness. Well, to be honest, I'm not a terribly serious person and although I have many opinions which I hold strongly, my function in *Points Of View* is not to express what I feel but to act in a way as a bridge between viewer and BBC, and indeed viewer and viewer. If the tone of the letters in any one week is cheerful rather than glum, that will be the mood of that week's programme.

There is a third element in the selection of letters and that is locality. We receive mail from the Orkneys and the Channel Islands, Belfast and Newcastle, Penzance and Hull, Rhyl and Dover, and everywhere in between. I feel that it helps people to know that their opinions are shared by others possibly several hundred miles away and try as far as possible to include letters from every part of the British Isles. Naturally, this can't happen in one ten-minute programme but in the course of the year I think it's true to say that practically every city, town and village in the UK has had a view expressed. Many people have written to say how much they like or dislike *Points of View* itself but these letters rarely get aired. The reason for this is simple: *Points Of View* is not about itself but about other programmes and while the letters are greatly appreciated (I print a selection in this book) to use them on the programme would smack of vanity and self-congratulation. So when people write to ask 'Why does nobody comment on *Points Of View*?' the answer is, they do.

Another question I am asked frequently is 'Are you censored?' The answer to that is no. I've been taken to task on more than one occasion for airing views critical of some performers or programmes, but I have never been told not to be critical of X or Y, nor, if I had, would I have taken much notice. I do exercise editorial discretion and will not print letters that are merely malicious or abusive. Often the writer does not comprehend the reasons why a presenter is off-form or a production is under par, and in any event I do not see my role as that of a purveyor of malice or senseless abuse.

As the majority of people who write to the programme are reasonable, whether in their praise or condemnation, I don't feel the need to expose people in the BBC who are, after all, my professional colleagues, to thoughtless attack. But mark the word thoughtless. I'm all for well-reasoned criticism and in fact *Points Of View* exists to air strongly-phrased critical opinions of BBC television programmes as well as ones favourable to the Corporation.

One last point, and we'll get to the letters. The question is often asked 'But does *Points Of View* do any good? Is any notice taken of what we write?' I believe it does do good and notice *is* taken. Programme makers and TV executives are only human and do react to criticism (even if they occasionally resent it). But it would be unrealistic to think that a criticism made on Friday will get something changed by the following Tuesday. But the BBC is a democratic organisation and is prepared to listen to anyone who has a point to make. While you keep writing they'll keep listening, and if in the process we can enjoy ourselves a little, well, nobody ever said that democracy shouldn't have a sense of humour.

Chapter One

PET HATES

Let's start with a few pet hates, some general, some particular. Mrs Lillian Hodge of Lostock Hall, Nr. Preston, comes straight to the point.

Dear BBC, Is it at all possible for you to employ one producer who is capable to produce an entertaining programme? We are so bored with the everlasting shooting, murder, and bed-ridden sex fanatics. In the present state of the world we have newspapers full of this sort of thing.

Mrs Hodge asks for more humorous programmes, '. . . something to laugh at.' But comedies get a hammering from Julia Watson of Leeds, whose letter I include, even if she does address me as Dear Brian.

Dear Brian, I am writing to give my Points Of View on BBC comedies such as *Terry And June*, and the dreadful *To The Manor Born*. What a load of despicable rubbish. I thought the BBC had far better comedies than the corny rubbish on ITV but now I'm not so sure. I'm afraid BBC you are falling as low as ITV. The majority of your comedies are middle-class rubbish or they are degrading the working class.

Cyril Beresford of Bristol is also concerned with the class issue.

Dear Barry Took, I don't have to tell you that 95% of all TV programmes are either rubbish or neo rubbish. . . I know the answer: People who write to the media in general are always members of the fussy middle class, whose ideas on entertainment, and for that matter on everything, are boring, dull and twee . . . you obviously take notice of them hence the lousy programmes.

I'm a member of the working class, a class which outnumber all the others 100 to 1, but never write in: except now . . .

I like football and think we should have more of it . . . I like cheeky comics like Bernard Manning . . . I like girl singers with low cut dresses . . . I like tough films, and plays showing rough cops knocking the living daylights out of thugs, and skinheads.

I don't like watching college boys trying to be comics by acting out their sixth form end of term sketches . . . I don't like aged actors and 'Personalities' playing parlour games . . . I am not interested in silly old women telling us how to train dogs . . . and, when I see these endless TV Drama and Theatre Awards and the people taking part who all try to be funny, and don't get laughs, I blush more than they do.

Just a few comments from my own, unrepresented class. ’

Harsh words from Bristol, and I'm tempted to say 'Nice one, Cyril'. Derek Heron of Washington, Tyne and Wear, is more succinct but more sweeping.

Dear Barry Took, I think *the BBC is a Load of Crap.*

Well at least Derek Heron doesn't hedge. Neither does Alex James of East Molesey, Surrey, who writes comprehensively on the subject of *Dallas.*

‘ Having made an early and thankful escape from the *Dallas* puerility, advance publicity cajoled me into returning for the sadistic delight of seeing the end of JR, and presumably, the tedious series. Unhappily, an imbecile curiosity has now compelled me to sit through two further boring episodes – mainly composed of hospital visits from his dreadful family and the droolings of his estranged wife.

But enough is enough. I no longer care who shot JR.

I only wish the public spirited assassin had been a better marksman, and that he or she had not wasted the remaining bullets in the revolver. Had his detestation of this appalling series been as great as my own, he could easily have disposed of the rest of the Ewings, leaving the ranch for sale, and the small screen available for the delights of a 1939 movie or a Fred Astaire and Ginger Rogers spectacular.

And now from the general to the particular, and three letters on the subject of buying, or rather not buying, British. The first is from John Bate of Prestatyn, Clwyd.

When watching last Wednesday's Parkinson Show, I was disgusted to see Dudley Moore playing a Japanese made piano, a Yamaha to be precise. The BBC are not setting a very good example to buy British, are they? If they *have* to use a foreign piano, why not one made in the Common Market? After all there are one or two quite good pianos made in West Germany.

The next letter is from F. Gutteridge of Stevenage.

Dear Barry Took, Why oh why cannot the BBC use a British made piano. In a recent chat programme – Parkinson – the camera zoomed in on the nameplate of a white Yamaha piano. I changed my Yamaha for a British made Chappell because it was a better piano – May I suggest that the BBC buys British?

The third letter is from K. M. Hodges of Sheffield.

During the programme *Tomorrow's World* on 30 October, part of the programme dealt with the measurement of stress in materials, as for example a motor cycle wheel. Why oh why show a Japanese motor cycle, why not a British motor cycle – aren't they good enough for the BBC?

There's no comment I can make about those letters as I'm not an expert on either pianos or motor bikes, but the last two illustrate what we in the *Points Of View* office have come to call the why oh why syndrome. More people use this phrase 'why oh why' when writing than any other. I wonder why? In fact, I'm tempted to say why oh why do they do it? Let's change the subject and print a few letters that have been written to *Points Of View*.
From James Coleman, Selly Oak, Birmingham.

Dear Barry Took,
I think that your program is one of the worst on the television.

Caroline Britten, aged 8, of Hull writes:

Dear Mr Took, I really detest *Points Of View*. I don't know how BBC can put the programme on television. The weather forecast is better than ten minutes of Barry Took.

and here is Rosalind Beck of Cardiff on the subject:

'Dear (and I use the term loosely) Barry, Why the heck has the BBC chosen to show such boring, monotonous rubbish as *Points Of View*. I'm all for free speech, but I don't think that boring, repetitive voices qualify in that category. In fact your programme is a pain. Normally I'm rather loath to get up and switch off the television but after lasting out one episode (?) of your programme, I suddenly became active, and whenever I hear the theme for *Points Of View*, I cringe, and jump up, turn off the telly, rush around the room banging my head against the wall, and tearing my hair out. Such is the effect that your programme has on me. It is worse torture than having your toenails pulled out and your arms chopped off simultaneously (I should imagine) and really it is a total waste of ten minutes of possible exciting viewing.

What made it worse this week – I was forced to watch it.

I would appreciate it if you could commit suicide. Failing that, emigrate to Australia.

Your Most Devoted and Faithful Fan,
Rosalind Beck.

Kirsty MacPhee, aged 11, of Stirling writes:

Barry Took,
I am writing to tell you that I think your programme is the worst on T.V. I would rather sit and watch a blank screen. I wish you would stop constantly grinning like a Cheshire cat, I really don't know what you find funny.

Graham Knight, aged 8, of Spennymoor, Co. Durham, says:

Dear Barry Took, I think you and your silly programme is absolutely pathetic – plus the BBC. I think the BBC should be called the RBC, which stands for the Rubbish Broadcasting Corporation. And for you – you big eared four eyed Monster, you and your silly programme go and don't come back any more because me and all my friends don't like you – so there.

And I've had uncomplimentary letters too! But seriously, I find it interesting how direct children can be. They leave you in no doubt as to their feelings, which makes their letters always a pleasure to read. But not so, says A. Grant, a pensioner from Wallasey, Merseyside.

> *Points Of View* is an interesting programme, but I think you give far too much prominence to letters from children. After all they don't buy TV licences, so why should we adults (who do) be inflicted with their comments?

The point there is that I use a percentage of letters from old and young and although children don't pay TV licences undoubtedly their parents do, and that gives them, in my opinion, right of access to the programme, and indeed to this book. But before we move on, or you think that I'm a masochist, I'd like to print a selection of letters which praise *Points Of View*. Sidney Denby of Wembley Park wrote in October –

> Dear Barry,
> for some inexplicable reason I like your programme but why must it be televised just at the time when I have to make our evening drink?

A question that has puzzled scientists for years. And how do you answer a plea like this from John Peterson of Glasgow –

> I wish to complain about the time the BBC shows your extremely entertaining programme, *Points Of View*. Could you change the show to any day but Friday as this is the night I have my driving lessons.

As Mr Peterson wrote that in September 1980, I sincerely hope he has now passed his driving test and can watch regularly. I also have my fans among the ladies. From Mrs X of Forest Gate, I received this letter.

Dear Barry,

I am quite surprised about people complaining about too much sex on BBC, but honestly when you come on the screen, twitching your nose, and curling your mouth at the corners – Wow! thats so sexy.

And Barbara Gallen of Mansfield wrote –

Dear Mr Took, I have resisted the impulse to write to *Points Of View* so many times, but my reserve was broken down this evening.

Your delightful 'camel face' should be hired out to the various political parties (without exception) as a person capable of enlivening the totally boring and banal Party Political Broadcasts.

And poetry yet – from G. and G.M.E. Wood of Eastbourne.

We are so very proud and fond of you
And your evening programme 'Points of View':
Your image in blue suit and tie of red
Entertains us well before time for bed;
We like your beardless rotund countenance,
With curling silvery thatch to enhance
Your dry, droll, Champagne wit, as you compere
Everyone's points of view for us to share.
We hope this letter you will dare to quote
As T.V's Best show, man – you have our vote!

And who would not be flattered by that?
Other letters comment on the look of the programme –

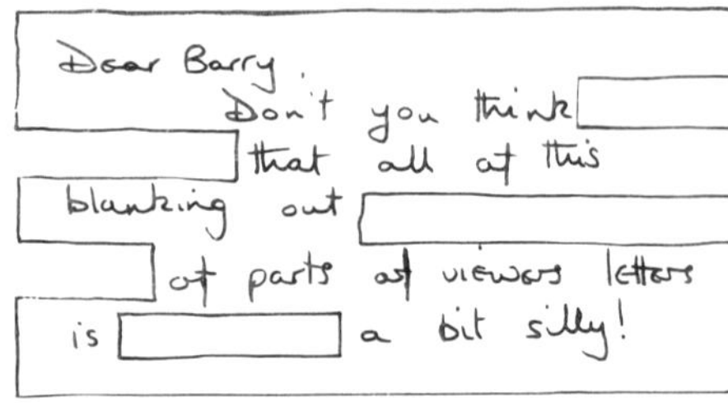
Dear Barry,
Don't you think
that all of this
blanking out
of parts of viewers letters
is a bit silly!

It may look a bit odd but there is method in our apparent madness. Often a viewer's point can be summed up in two or three lines, so in the early days the letters were rewritten, but that clearly lacked authenticity and was dropped. We then tried circling the phrase used in the original letter, like so

Dear Mr Took,
I really like *Last of The Summer Wine* but I can't stand 'canned' laughter especially when they're laughing at something on film. Since when did a field of cows have a cackling audience?

Without distorting the point of the original letter, we highlighted what was said. But it looked scruffy. So now we use the present method and on the whole it works. There have been a number of subtle changes since we began – a different backing to the tiny set, a new chair and by the autumn of 1980 we dropped the very clever and ingenious opening title sequence. The reason was that it took 18 seconds and I felt that the time could be better used reading an extra letter or two. It was a point noticed and appreciated by many. This letter from A. E. Tyrrill of Faversham, Kent, being typical.

Dear *Points Of View*, It's time you received a bouquet!

How pleasant it is to see a programme go straight in – no dallying with musical intros, no desert scenes with flutes, and no high falutin' nonsense with rostrum cameras piling on agonies of waiting for you to begin!!

Which brings us on to the vexed question of background music, sound effects, studio audiences, and other matters that produce a constant stream of correspondence.

Chapter Two

'ALL THAT DAMNED MUSIC'

It's a stock joke in films and television when looking at the rough cut of a programme before putting on the sound effects and atmosphere to the soundtrack to say, 'It'll be fine when we've added the music.' But this is not the view of many of our correspondents. Dr K. A. Chapman of Somerton, Somerset, writes forcibly on the subject.

> Why the devil have we always to put up with some damn silly tune (usually a bad one) bumbling away with fatuous imbecility as 'background' to every item on TV? One can't even enjoy a natural history programme without one – as though birds, flowers and insects lived their lives against a non-stop accompaniment of sixteenth rate Vaughan Williams!

Thus the good doctor; so too Miss E. Foster of Barnet.

> Why must there always be incidental music when a documentary is shown? It would be most surprising if at a lecture (not on television) an orchestra or pianist persisted in playing whenever the lecturer paused for breath, or illustrated his lecture in some way. Sometimes on television the music even continues during the commentary. I would think the majority of viewers do not need to be distracted and could bear a few moments of silence.

There must *be* a reason why music is added. It certainly *can* help in the creation of atmosphere, but not a bit of it cry our correspondents who write more often and more vehemently about background music and 'canned' laughter (of which more later) than on almost any other subject. Clarence Winchester of Haywards Heath really takes the battle to the enemy with his rousing defence of silence.

Can *nothing* still be done – in spite of many protests – to kill the background 'music' (so called!) that overwhelms dialogue and ruins otherwise peaceful scenes where silence or only Nature's sounds prevail?

Do producers on all channels believe that the hideous and depressing moans are **enjoyed** and that without them we should die of heart failure in this Age of Noise? Sack the lot, I cry, including the moan makers and those who compose (loud cynical laughter!) the moans!

And G. Bastin of Jersey, Channel Islands, aware that he is not the only one to detest 'Background Music', comments –

If I am one of many who would like this cut out – why have you not done so?

The subject rouses strong emotions and one can sympathise with Mrs Kirk of Spilsby, Lincolnshire, when she says –

Dear Sirs, Please spare a thought for we deaf people. Need the background music and clapping be so loud. We have to turn our hearing aids up to hear what people say and then the blast nearly deafens us. I have to sit with my hand on my hearing aid – up and down all night. Surely it need not be so loud, and why so much clapping?

That was a small selection from the thousands of letters that *Points Of View* has received on the subject, and if it's not music or applause that bothers many viewers it's the laughter of the studio audience. R. Carson of Newton Abbot, Devon, writes in strong terms but is, in my view, both fair and accurate.

Dear Mr Took, In the interest of millions of TV viewers, cannot something be done whereby we may be spared the full blast of 'audience laughter' during comedies?

It has become intolerable and distinctly tiresome. Let the studio audience laugh by all means – as it acts as a stimulant to the artists, but surely it is not beyond the ingenuity of the technicians to 'fade out' at least 80% of this raucous laughter in order that we, the viewing public, may fully enjoy the comedies, and provide our laughter. ’

The answer here lies with the director or producer involved. It is physically possible for the sound engineer to strike a balance between what the microphones pick up in the studio and what the viewer receives at home, but all too often the constant loud guffaws thought to be necessary by light entertainment producers can be profoundly irritating.
Rex Wood of Wolverhampton waxes satirical on the subject.

Dear Barry Took,
(Ha-ha-ha) How do you manage to conduct your programme without laughter? (Clap-clap-clap)
It is quite disturbing to me (Ha-ha-ha-hee-hee) that there are still programmes being shown with no accompanying intermittent (Chuckle) laughter or applause. (Ha-ha-ha-ha-clap-clap-rumble)
How on earth can we viewers (Ha-ha) be expected to know when something is amusing (Chortle) if we are given no guidance? (Clap-clap-clap-clap)
Do get into line Barry (He-hee-ho-ho) and include some taped laughter in your programme. (Clap-clap-clap-shriek-clap-ho-ho-clap)

Yours sincerely,
Rex (Chuckle) Wood.

P.S. Couldn't some of the serious programmes have a few sighs and groans? (Agh-oo-ah)

As a matter of fact, in the early days of *Points Of View*, we received a similar letter and the producer added a 'laughter track' to my reply. Needless to say the effect was ghastly, as it was meant to be, but such was my pavlovian response to laughter and applause,

I did actually perk up when I heard it. A curious, slightly unnerving experience.
In the normal course of events, *Points Of View* is, as Frankie Howerd might say, 'titterless', a point appreciated by John Exley of Stockport, Cheshire.

> I find your programme very refreshing – and it's free from the *'laugh machine'*.
>
> Many good comedy programmes are spoilt by bursts of loud laughter, obviously not from a 'live' audience, these staccato bursts spoil the entertainment and I frequently turn off the sound or change the channel. Often the *'Machine'* is at a higher sound level than the programme it is covering – why spoil entertainment? There's not all that much to laugh at these days.

Here's Reginald Ruegg of Stevenage on the subject.

> Dear Barry,
> Isn't it about time the use of canned laughter was scrapped?
> In my opinion it ruins completely many comedy shows and I am sure this dislike is shared by the majority of viewers.
>
> It doesn't improve or bolster up a poor script, in fact, it has the opposite effect.
> In view of this, could not the Radio Times carry out an opinion poll and should the masses agree please could this inane, false laughter be left out of future scripts.
> One final comment. How different and enjoyable is the response and well earned laughter from a live audience.

While most of the so-called 'canned laughter' does come from the audience in the studio at the recording of a comedy show, it is no secret that a small laugh can be 'hyped' into a roar of laughter. It's against the rules (the BBC rules, that is) but it *is* done.
On behalf of the many viewers who have complained and still do complain, regularly, may I make a plea to my colleagues in Light Entertainment for moderation.

In that most excellent of recent comedy series, *Yes Minister*, there was one extraordinary continuity lapse. The Permanent Under Secretary's tie changed from paisley to maroon with white spots, and back again within seconds – and we had letters from all over the country pointing this out. When we showed the offending sequence I thought it would be a good idea if between clips I too changed ties from spots to stripes and back again. An innocent enough joke, but it provoked this response from Miss J. Pattinson of South Wirral.

Dear Barry Took,
Last week you mentioned a magic tie on the programme "Yes Minister," well that's not the only programme with magic ties hanging around. Last week on your very own programme, your very own ties changed.
Look before you leap!

It surprises me how sharp-eyed our viewers are, and how they notice the smallest lapse in continuity. In October 1980, Mr G. Knight of Rhyl, Clwyd, wrote –

My wife and I both noticed that in *Terry and June* shown on October 3rd that Terry put an apron on the hall table and went out to work with June.

The next shot was of Terry coming home from work, but no apron.

We can only assume that they have a housekeeper that we never see.

And here's J. R. Kinchen of Bedhampton, Hants, on a boo-boo that appeared in *Mackenzie*.

The mistake that I noticed was the Morris 1000 van which came to a halt outside a building in a street which was a much later model than 1955, the year in which the play was supposed to be set. All Morris Minors made prior to mid 1956, had a two piece windscreen fitted, but the Morris 1000 van in your opening scene had only a one piece windscreen, as displayed on all Morris Minors made from mid 1956 to the end of production in 1970/71.

And on the subject of anachronisms, E. C. Thornett of Redditch, Worcestershire wrote in July 1980 about –

> The programme *The Moon Stallion*. The period long before the motor car! Please end the concern for us at number 43. When Diana bids farewell to the Moon Stallion does he disappear from the top of the hill to gallop off to 'Luton Airport' to catch that jet aircraft that flies over at about 30,000 feet leaving a super vapour trail?

And finally, in this section, a comment on *The Onedin Line*. Stuart Selwyn of Wembley spotted this anomaly in the otherwise impeccable series, and wrote to tell me about it.

> I noted with regret that even that excellent, and normally lavish production, THE ONEDIN LINE, has fallen prey to the creeping cancer of petty economies.
>
> Whilst applauding the motives of the estimable Dunwoody in encouraging the new MRS. James to come close to the fire after her dreadful experience (SUN. 28th's. episode), it is surely straining our "willing suspension of disbelief" to find her staring wistfully at an empty grate?

Chapter Three

ECONOMIES AND TIMING

If the BBC are conscious of the need for economies in these difficult times the viewers are equally aware of the need to cut back even if their ideas are not quite on the scale the Director General has in mind. Mr Eddie Richley of Tulse Hill asks –

In these days of economy is there any good reason that in *Grandstand* on Saturday afternoons every latest football score is handed to Frank Bough on a pink foolscap sheet of paper.

Have they not heard of pads of a smaller size?

Mr Frank McNeil of Glasgow has another view of how money can be saved –

Dear Barry Took, In these days of economic decline when the BBC is supposedly short of money, is it really necessary to send Shirley Bassey around the world to sing a few songs and wiggle her hips a few times? Surely a vast amount of money is spent on these pointless excursions.

On Monday 6 October in a forty-five-minute show she appeared in about ten different costumes. I lost count after eight.

Reg Hamilton of Meadowfield, Lanark, got the number of Shirley Bassey's dresses exactly.

Dear *Points Of View*, While watching the Shirley Bassey Show on Monday evening I counted the number of changes of outfits she wore viz. nine in number.

Miss Bassey looks delightful in her gorgeous dresses and her show is excellent but I feel, if the BBC provides her clothes, this is one area where there could be a reduction in expenditure. Two or three dresses would be sufficient.

And G. Y. Messenger of Oxford has yet another suggestion regarding Miss Bassey.

Dear Barry Took,

Does the fabulous Shirley Bassey use "super glue".

The reason I ask is that despite numerous costume changes during her recent BBC 2 shows her ear-rings remain the same.

Perhaps it's a BBC economy measure – would it not be cheaper to change the ear-rings and keep the same gown??

As you can see, our correspondents have no shortage of ingenious ideas for 'cutbacks', even if many of them are tongue in cheek. But laughter dies when it comes to the subject of the licence fee. I print here one of the many letters received on the subject. This is from L. R. C. Bailey of Pound Hill, West Sussex.

MY FAMILY AND I ARE SICK TO DEATH OF HAVING TO PAY YOUR <u>EXTORTIONATE</u> T.V. LICENCE FEE, FOR SOMETHING WE DON'T

BENEFIT FROM. ALL THE BEST PROGRAMMES ARE ON I.T.V., AND THEY EARN THEIR MONEY ON THEIR OWN MERITS, WHICH IS MORE THAN WE CAN SAY FOR B.B.C. RUBBISH.

IF THIS LICENCE DOESNT GO BY NEXT YEAR, MY TELEVISION WILL, AND THE SOONER, YOU LOT GO OUT OF BUSINESS THE BETTER.

I DON'T EXPECT THIS LETTER TO BE SHOWN ON POINTS OF VIEW YOU WOULDN'T DARE!

Well, Mr Savage, your letter wasn't read on the programme but does appear here, so I suppose you could say that it's a draw.
But now a cry, or rather a series of cries from the heart about the *timing* of programmes. Miss G. E. Leigh of Peterborough makes her point succinctly –

Dear Barry

Why do the B.B.C. put programmes on so late at night.

Miss Irene Greer, aged 11, of Rutherglen, Glasgow, writes at greater length.

Dear Barry,
I am a great lover of the art of dance. I think that the B.B.C.'s idea of putting on classical ballet at all hours of the night is absolutely ridiculous— and that is putting it mildly! For instance Swan Lake was on a few weeks ago, half past ten until well after twelve o'cklock, that is Ludicrous. Now the firebird is on which I would really love to see, and what time is it on at? 10·50 until 11·20. I am sick fed up missing all the ballet's that I would love to see because they are on so late. If the B.B.C. think that adults are the only ones who love classical ballet then they are very wrong. I would be more than gratefull if the B.B.C. would think about this before putting Ballets on at such stupid times

Parents too felt indignant at the placing of BBC 2's 1980 Ballet season. Mrs W. J. Moltag of Teversham, Cambs, for instance.

Our daughter is a ballet fanatic and is furious that we will not allow her to stay up and watch the ballet shown on BBC 2 at 11 o'clock, however we and I am sure, a great many other parents consider this too late for schoolchildren to stay up during the weekdays.

Please tell me why this programme cannot be shown earlier in the evening. Is Nureyev considered obscene and unfit for family viewing?

And we also received this letter – there was no address alas, and, I suspect, signed pseudonymously 'Swanhilda Lake'.

Dear Mr. Took,

I would like to express my disappointment at having to decline Mr. Nureyev's "Invitation To The Dance".

Owing to the programme being broadcast at such a late hour, I, and almost certainly other Ballet fans have to forego the pleasure of viewing this particular series.

If and when it is repeated (which I sincerely hope it is), perhaps the BBC will take into consideration the number of people (young and old) who would like to see the series, and hopefully broadcast it at a more suitable hour.

Not only lovers of classical dancing are upset when dance programmes are on late. We received a stack of mail when the recent series of *Come Dancing* was aired rather later than might be expected. This letter from Karen Lloyd of Shrewsbury is typical of many.

Dear Barry Took,

I think the BBC should hide themselves away with shame, for putting that fantastic programme "COME-DANCING" on at the stupid time of 10.40pm, I'm sure every dancer in England shares my view. especially the children dances who have to go to school the next day, how dissapointing for them not to see their stars in beautiful dresses dance away, to that super music.

It's not only dancing that's on later than people wish. Every late night programme brings its quota of complaint. As Anne Graham of Ilkley, West Yorks, says –

Could you possibly get someone to explain the logic behind placing so many good programmes very late at night? It happens so often, but I am particularly incensed this week to find yet another Woody Allen film relegated to the middle of the night. How many people will watch so far into the night? Is the BBC trying to change the nation's sleeping habits?

There must be a very good reason why this type of film cannot be screened at, say, ten o'clock, but I cannot fathom it.

Beverley Randall of Abertillery, Gwent, also complains of the lateness of her favourite programmes.

It really annoys me when I have to watch two of my favourite programmes – *Film 80*, and Parkinson – with matchsticks holding my eyes open.

Please could you use your influence on the programme controller and the D.G. (not Terry Wogan) to transmit these programmes at a more reasonable hour, so that I no longer wake up in the morning with bags and dark circles under my eyes.

In the matter of programme schedules, I'm afraid Beverley Randall overestimates my influence, and Sally Bourns of Sydenham SE26 wonders about it.

Dear Mr Took, I do not know if you have any influence over the timing of programmes, but every time I get hooked on good serials like *The Brothers*, *The Onedin Line*, and last of all *Dallas* they get changed to church time on Sunday, and I never see them again. I suppose I should be thankful to see Penelope Keith in *To The Manor Born*, which I am. Would you please ask the BBC to have repeats of these good serials on a weekday evening, excluding Wednesday.

And if programmes are not too late they're too early, as witness this letter from Karen Crombie of Duns in Berwickshire.

I am writing to say I think the B.B.C are ROTTEN. They've put "Heidi" on at 4.40 and I don't get home from school until 4.45 so I'll miss the first five minutes of every episode.

Chapter Four

NAUGHTY BITS

Are the BBC too permissive or not permissive enough? The fors and againsts explicit sex and bad language come out surprisingly even, which means, I suppose, that the BBC gets it about right.

Here are a selection of views expressed on the subject that we've received since *Points Of View* started. Mr McPherson of Port St Mary, Isle of Man, has written a letter with which many people will agree. He says –

'Life as portrayed on the TV screen has lost all its dignity. We appear as slaves to drink and nudity. The continual reachings for the bottle makes folk look spineless, a view of our nation that terrifies me.

My eyes are tired of nakedness. Females have thrown overboard all their hidden charm and mystery. An ecstatic embrace is far more telling in a love scene than bed and mouthing. Please let our animal nature lie behind the intriguing closed door, and give back to modern Man his dignity and reticence.'

Back in February 1980, the BBC showed a film *The Sicilian Clan*. Next day, Mrs Jill Chandler, of Deal in Kent, sat down and wrote to me.

'Dear Mr Took, I feel so strongly about the BBC's error of judgement last night that I must write.

Last night my two children and myself sat down to watch what we thought was going to be a crime thriller. *The Sicilian Clan* started at 7.15 and ended at 9 p.m. and it never occurred to me that there would be anything in it to cause offence or embarrassment. Imagine my feelings when, not too far into the story, the hero (or anti-hero) is seen in bed with a topless prostitute. My nine-year-old son was delighted and fell about in his armchair. My rapidly developing twelve-year-old daughter was not amused at his antics and I tried to laugh it off. Further on we were treated to a whole army of topless ladies, causing my son further amusement and my daughter more embarrassment. When, therefore, approximately half an hour before the end, we find a lady stretched out on the beach stark naked (admittedly on her stomach) and the hero purposefully striding up the beach towards her, the time had come for the OFF button to be employed. My son made a hullaballoo, as did my daughter as we were well on into the story by then, but I really could not risk sitting through writhing bodies in the sand and all its implications.

I thought it was BBC policy to put 'adult' programmes like this on after 9 o'clock and how, for heaven's sake, did this one slip through the net? I am not a prude and before having children was as liberal in my ideas and TV and film watching as the next woman, but I firmly believe that children ought to be protected from overt nudity and sexuality on the TV screen (also violence) and cannot protest too strongly at what must have been a temporary aberration on the part of the programme organisers. ’

I think that Mrs Chandler is right when she uses the words 'temporary aberration' and says that *The Sicilian Clan* 'slipped through the net', and being the father of a twelve-year-old daughter myself understand the problems of being suddenly faced with a scene I don't want her to see. The trouble is that censorship is often worse than what it seeks to censor. I rather take the point of Clifford Gulliver of Saltash, Cornwall, who wrote in October 1980 –

‘ Dear Barry Took, May I mention the 'statutory scene'? You know, the one where a naked couple bounce on a bed and chew one another's faces.

This scene is becoming obligatory, for the sake of Art and Realism of course, in Romantic Plays, Message Plays, and even Whodunnits. Where will it pop up next? Maybe that nice Weathergirl was wise to quit when she did.

Soon, I suppose, we shall have *Romans in Britain* on TV with nice big close ups but after that what will the poor writers and directors be able to do to keep audiences switched on? Shall we go down in history, not as the people who went to the Moon, but as the ones who actually succeeded in making sex boring?

But you never know. Perhaps it's just one of Mother Nature's ingenious devices for controlling a species which is reaching plague proportions. Ask David Attenborough.

Yours sincerely,

Clifford Gulliver.

PS For heaven's sake don't let the BBC put a girl into your programme. The scene wouldn't suit your noble configuration.

PPS I can just see you saying, 'Oh, I don't know though' with a wicked look.

Well, it's a thought Mr Gulliver, it's a thought. Miss P. Sinclair of Stoke on Trent puts the whole thing in a nutshell –

After watching a succession of films, comedies etc., e.g. *Night Moves, Not the Nine O'Clock News, Breezy*, showing an abundance of nudity, my mother and I think BBC should stand for the Boobs and Bums Channel!

But does it affect the young? Adam Bourne, aged 9, of Cranbrook, Kent, gets quite cross.

Dear Barry Took,
We watch T.V. every night but nearly all the programmes have kissing on, please is there any programmes without kissing, kissing, kissing.

If it isn't kissing, it's swearing. Mrs Christine Whittall of Broadstone, Dorset, asks:

Please can you find out why there has to be so much swearing on television?

Well, Mrs Whittall, I suppose it's thought to add realism to a production. After all, in real life people *do* swear; in fact it's become part of the texture of urban life, and after all swearing is meaningless – ugly yes, but literally senseless. However, Mrs Whittall continues her letter in a vein echoed by many people who write to *Points Of View*.

We find that what would be good programmes are spoilt by constant swearing. *Juliet Bravo*, *Angels*, and *Mackenzie* to name but a few. Even *All Creatures Great and Small* slip them in, so series that we would otherwise enjoy we switch off. Not only for our children's sakes, but because it leaves a nasty taste in our mouths too. Why is it that the swearing is in British films? You don't hear it in *Kojak*, *Starsky and Hutch*, or *Petrocelli*, do you?

Ah, but Kojak and the rest are concerned with real violence, not the verbal kind. Still, swearing on TV does upset many people. Shauna Tuck, aged 11, of Swanley, Kent, among them.

Dear Mr Took, Why is there such bad language on TV? After your programme I thought back to *The Dawson Watch* – the language is unbelievable. Luckily my brother aged 7 was not watching it. *Juliet Bravo* is a good programme except for the language. All TV programmes could be good but it's the bad language that spoils them.

Susan Howarth of Salford feels much the same.

I am 12 years old and I am disgusted at some of the swearing that goes on in serials and plays on T.V. quite early at night.

Could this not be stopped by putting a 'beep' in everytime a swear word is used.

If every swear word was 'beeped' the effect would be TV in morse code. I spent much of a recent *Points Of View* programme on the subject of bad language on television and received a sharp rap over the knuckles from Carolyn Vincent of Swaffham, Norfolk.

Dear Mr Took, I expect by now your own family has long since left home, and are no longer your responsibility.

I have three sons, and my husband and I are endeavouring to bring them up in the best way we can.

We all took exception to your jocular manner over the criticism yesterday on the BBC's excessive use of bad language recently.

It is true as you say, we can turn the set off, but what is the use of a television when it's never on!?

We all enjoy watching as a family, and we feel the BBC should be aware that *many* people (not just a few cranks) find bad language distasteful.

Of course I take Mrs Vincent's point but my position is simple. I am not a censor, nor is it my job to moralise. Incidentally, all my family have not left home and I believe that I am a responsible parent. As for being jocular, well, so are many of our correspondents. Colin R. Barrett of Milton Keynes for example.

What's all this fuss about sex on television?

If it came to a choice between having a war film that praised senseless violence, or sex, I'd choose to have sex every time. Wouldn't you?

So what's wrong with sex on the television? (or anywhere else, for that matter!)

Mrs Luanne Stockwell of Bury St Edmunds, on the subject of the series *Mackenzie*, writes if not with tongue in cheek then at least with one eyebrow raised –

Oh dear, Mr Took, oh dear! I was once persuaded to watch *Another Bouquet* on ITV and a dead bore it was too, for in the two episodes I actually stayed with, it seemed that the only person *not* having an affair was the baby!

Now I see the lady who wrote it is at it again, but on BBC 1 this time. A delicate little piece called *Mackenzie* and already the screen's full of twitching buttocks.

With everything so adulterated one trembles for *Gardeners' Question Time.*

Again on the subject of *Mackenzie*, I received this letter from Mr M. M. F. J. of Edinburgh.

I feel compelled to inform you that there are viewers who are not disgusted by 'sex on the television' in such programmes as *Mackenzie*. I personally would prefer to see more sex on programmes after 9.00 or 10.00 o'clock, after all that is 'adult viewing' time.

From the letters you received last week, one would imagine that the British public is composed of sex-scared prudes.

The last word on the subject goes to D. M. Brown of Sleaford, Lincs.

Having just watched this week's episode of *Mackenzie*, on BBC 1, I feel that I really must bring to your attention what must be television's 'pun of the week' when, in a remorseful mood, Diana turned to Piers and asked 'Why does sex screw everything up?'

Chapter Five

THE OTHER SIDE

It's amazing how many people still regard the BBC as the 'enquire within' about all television, whether BBC or ITV. Perhaps I should have sent the letters I regularly receive on the subject of commercial television productions to the IBA. It might have helped their deliberations leading up to the award of the new franchises. Oscar Rogers of Coulsdon, Surrey, sets the tone of this section.

Dear Barry, I have a suggestion. Why don't you get the guy that does your programme to stretch your programme to cover ITV as well as BBC, as most of the worst programmes appear on this – so called television channel – How about it?

'So called' or not ITV is a fact of life and comments come in all shapes and sizes. I particularly enjoyed reading this letter from Aileen Garve of Dunfermline, which I received shortly after I'd started doing *Junior Points Of View* on the Saturday morning marathon, Swap Shop.

Dear Swap shop,

This letter is all about give us a clue.
I like it.

It is about when they tell you what the clue is they shood not tell us the clue becauese it gives away the clue and then we cood get the clue at home.
I wish we cood fix it.

Not so happy about one of Thames Television's offerings is Mr W. G. Symons of Ruislip, Middlesex.

Cowboys – I should think the director, producer, and all those connected with it represent the *Cowboys*.

I've never seen so much drivel and rubbish in all my life.

But in case anyone from Thames reads this and thinks I'm putting the boot in, I reproduce, in the interests of balance, this letter from Emma Cox of Whitehaven.

> I am over the moon about the BBC's programme Cowboys. I sit on a Wednesday and whatch this hilarious programme which gives the hysterics. This really does brighten up my wednesday evening. come on the BBC more of this great stuff.

Ellen Reardon of Poplar E.14 is 18 and writes as follows:

> Dear Barry, Whilst watching one of my favourite TV programmes, *The Professionals*, I felt indignant with a realisation that moved me to write to you!
>
> With a definite sense of justice, I must point out the undeniable fact that Lewis Collins in his portrayal of 'Bodie' is being denied his due. It seems to me that he never receives what is surely deserved in the way of female attention. He is in fact deprived! He is adorably handsome and some beauty ought to be cast to tickle his fancy – he deserves this at least.
>
> With best wishes,
>
> Ellen Reardon.
>
> PS I am 18 years old and shall be intrigued to find out, if fortunate enough to have this read out on your proggi, which of your female voices will be used.

Well, Ellen, you didn't make the programme but here you are in print, so you can read your letter in any voice you choose. Here's a

letter from someone who didn't stop to think about which channel he was watching. Actually the show Lawrence Jones of Folkestone was commenting on back in September 1980 was produced by London Weekend Television.

> I am writing to say how much I enjoyed the programme called "The worst of It'll be alright on the night". All through the programme I was rolling up with laughter. As soon as it had finished I ran up stairs and started to write this letter.
>
> I must say the B.B.C. do turn out some excellent comedy programmes, what with "Not the nine o'clock news" and "The return of the pink panther", with Peter Sellers.

The same Company produced the series *Holding The Fort* – a fact that Mrs Joyce Peach of Burton Latimer knew perfectly well when she wrote this.

> Dear Barry Took,
> *Holding The Fort*
> Best comedy since *Not The Nine O'Clock News* – Trouble is I have to miss last ten minutes of it because of *you*!!!
> Yours,
> Joyce Peach (Mrs)
> PS Your eyes fascinate me – is it make up or the 'specs'?
> PPS Don't get excited – I am fat and 50!

Mrs Peach, I'm not getting excited. I'm fat and fifty-three. And here's another letter from Northamptonshire, from Miss J. Dillon of Kettering.

Just a note about Glenda Brownlow of *Crossroads*. Do you think all *Crossroads* fans might like to start a fund for Glenda to buy her a new handbag.

I feel the yellow plastic one she carries with whatever she wears is wearing a bit thin. Do you think she only has one bag. Have any other watchers noticed this?

Having only watched *Crossroads* by accident I can't really comment.

On the subject of repeats, D. A. Cocks of Rugby makes an interesting point –

Although at first sight it appears that the BBC shows more repeats, if you take into account the fact that each independent company bores us to tears with approximately 360 hours of immature advertisements annually, most of which are repeated not once or twice, but dozens of times, you begin to get a more realistic picture.

Additionally the BBC doesn't have the gall to insult our intelligence with such pathetic trash as *Crossroads*, *Soap*, etc. etc., the list is endless.

Keep up the good work, BBC.

Melissa Griffiths of Wrexham, Clwyd, also on the subject of advertisements – or rather one in particular –

I am writing to complain about the "Whiskas" advert. At the end of every one of these adverts it always says, "8-10 owners said their cats preferred it. It never shows the 2 owners who dont recommend it. Please would you talk to the 2 owners who dont recommend "Whiskas" and ask them if they would do the advert instead of the other eight.

There's not much I can do about it Melissa but it seems a good idea. Let's say that imitation is the sincerest form of flattery and leave it at that.

I've received dozens of letters praising and criticising ITV programmes, but the most constructive letter on the subject came from Andrew Ryding of Chorley, Lancs.

'Dear Barry, On Friday 5th of September, I was browsing through the *Radio* and *TV Times* to see what I could watch the following day. At 7.30 on ITV there was a James Bond Film. I was quite pleased when I saw this because I happen to like him. My pleasure soon changed when I saw that on BBC 1 there was an adventure film at 8.30. I was extremely annoyed because I would have liked to have seen both the films.

I think that the BBC and ITV should *co-operate* a bit more, rather than compete.'

Chapter Six

OUT OF THE MOUTHS OF BABES . . .

I know I've quoted many letters from children in this selection of *Points Of View*, but I so enjoy receiving letters from children I make no apology for reprinting yet more in this section.

Their views cover a wide variety of subject and are, on the whole, well worth reading. For instance, this from Helen Steel aged 10.

> I like everything just like my Dad even if he dose not like the thing he stil watches it. Mam says the box rules our life but i think thats stupid.

Mark Purnell, aged 8½, of Melksham brings a blinding logic to bear on the subject of *Star Trek*.

> On Star Trek They say at the beginning "To boldly go where no man has gone before" But when they reach places, People are always already there!

Jonathan Chamberlain, aged $8\frac{3}{4}$, of Derby also wrote to me on the subject of *Star Trek*.

My brother and
I think Star Trek To night
was a waste of time.
Grown ups Kissing each other
and saying sloppy things
Ugh it was dreadful
Please give us more fight-
-ing

Susan Chapman, aged 8, of Mathern, Nr Chepstow, Gwent, clearly enjoys action too –

> I think that K9 should not be taken out of *Doctor Who*. If he is taken out I will be very upset because he makes it more thrilling when he breaks down, and shoots people, and things shoot out of his nose.

Children's complaints about television are various. Here's Sam Southwick of London W.12.

I'd like to say, that my mother and my grand mother and myself enjoy *MASTERMIND* , but we all think that the lady's ware horrible dresses. Please could you ask the B B C not to let the lady's ware the dresses. I'm quite sure the B B C has got nicer one's!

While Colin Greenberg of Edgware, Middlesex, is 'disgusted'.

> My father has just paid £35 for a colour television licence and I was disgusted on Sunday afternoon when both BBC channels were broadcasting Black and White Films of 1935 and 1937 vintage.
>
> Have the BBC forgotten what a colour television is for.
>
> PS THREE CHEERS FOR RADIO!!

Sue Norris of Yoxall, Staffs, is also disgusted – and at great length –

I am Fourteen years old and I'm despairing with the BBC. Why Oh, Why have the BBC got to put all the funniest programs on BB2 at 9.00 to 10.00. For example:

Monday – Rhoda.

It's so good!!!

Tuesday – Butterflies

Well I've never laughed so much...

– "Not the Nine 'o' clock News"

This is what really gets me mad. I love this program. It's so crude. AND IT'S ON TO LATE!!!

Wednesday - M.A.S.H.

Give me more!!!

I do wish you'd put these on earlier. Say in the place of Panarama. What a bore!! If adults want to watch it, why not put it on later?

Not all children complain, of course. This letter from Alice Prendergast of Cardiff is typical of many.

> I thought I simply must write saying how much I enjoyed Johnny Ball's series "Think of a number". It made me think a little more about my surroundings. Thank-you BBC, lets have a new series soon!.

And here's one of those unanswerable questions which comes with, I suspect, a touch of Lancashire wit. It comes from Jill Fielden (aged 8) of Rochdale.

> Why, why, why does Richard Baker have to clench his hands so tightly that his knuckles go white and his fingers go purple? Is he nervous or are his trousers too tight?

A more serious point (one shared by many I need hardly say) is made by Michelle Scull of St Brelade, Jersey, C.I.

> I think the programme *Grandad* is spoilt by all that laughing going on and a cough in the middle of a sentence. Why can't the BBC put it right like it was before with no audience. Then we can laugh when we want.

But here's a cry from the heart if I ever heard one. It comes from Annelise Brilli of Hove.

> I envy the presenters of the Blue Peter programe because of the opportunities they get to go to places. Can you tell me how I can get a Job on Blue peter.

Well, I'm not sure I know the answer, or if by the time Miss Brilli is old enough she'll still feel the same way. Children's tastes change, often from week to week, and it's a tribute to BBC Children's Department that they keep so many children of all ages interested, informed and amused. But how would you answer *this* from Duncan Gregory, aged 9?

> Dear sir
>
> Why do you have so many <u>LOVE</u> programs on T.V.

Chapter Seven

JOLLY GOOD SPORTS

On *Points Of View* we get more letters on the subject of sport than on any other. Sportsmen and women, by the very nature of their enthusiasm, seem to be more active correspondents than people who write on other subjects, although it's fair to say the *anti*-sport lobby are just as vociferous. Mr D. R. Wardle of Southsea, writing on behalf of himself and a Miss Gail Sinclair, says –

“Gail and I have got so tired of having sport *rammed* down our throats on all three channels – frequently at the same time – that we decided to find out what percentage of viewing time is taken up on this subject. Did you know that on a good week – I mean with less coverage than usual – That 43% of afternoon viewing and 27% of evening viewing over a seven day period was taken up with sport.

Do you at the BBC think that all the British population are complete illiterate morons. We're fed up watching footballers kissing and cuddling, boring commentary with frequent replays discussing whether it could possibly have been a goal if the wind had been blowing easterly instead of westerly.

For goodness sake, we pay for our licence, so let's have 'fair play' on this.”

Fair play it is then, as I hope to demonstrate by quoting this letter from Glen Griffiths of Norwich.

“Dear Barry Took, Generally a placid person I find myself forced to put a pen to paper in defence of the silly allegation that too many hours of television is devoted to sport.

Having carefully taken into account the total number of television hours per week, I estimate that *only* 10% is actually given to sport! Surely no one can seriously consider this percentage so outrageous?

I would suggest that those against sport, either switch off, turn over, or better still *participate*. But I don't doubt that hearing the very word, 'participate' 100,000 viewers would probably collapse! Healthy body, healthy mind. Think about it! Please.

Here's Mrs D. S. Allnutt of High Wycombe, Bucks, still on the subject of sport on all channels.

Whilst I understand that you cannot be held responsible for Independent Television viewing, it seems to me that we should be able to expect a rather wider choice than that offered by BBC 1 and BBC 2. I understood that the second BBC channel was meant to enhance and widen the scope of viewing available to your audience. I can only assume that you have interpreted this to mean that you can now double the amount of sports coverage so that you can, therefore, attract the boxing enthusiast as well as the golfer.

Of course, I may be wrong, but I am sure that I am not the only person amongst your audience who thinks that a choice between Sport, Sport or Sport is no choice at all.

When *Rugby Special* was moved from Sunday to Saturday, it raised a storm of protest, as this letter from Lyn Horscroft of Bristol indicates.

What a ridiculous day and time to change *Rugby Special* – 7.15 p.m. Saturdays!! Does the BBC not appreciate that a *large* number of *Rugby Special fans* are also Rugby players. My husband is an ardent fan of the programme, but is also Bar Secretary of his local Rugby Club and is seldom home before 8 p.m. on a Saturday, following a match. He must be just one of hundreds of Rugby players who are now unable to watch one of their favourite programmes of the week.

Mrs Margaret Bradley of Lewes would agree.

What do the *powers that be* think they are doing by putting *Rugby Special* on *Saturday* evening, of all times! Do they not know that any self respecting Rugby player is still at his club or his opposition's at that time?

I never knew that so many ladies were so keen on Rugby – but these letters are not untypical.

But from the ovoid to the round ball and soccer. Michael Norris writes at length, and amusingly –

Whilst I cannot claim any experience or talent for programme scheduling, as a Sunday morning footballer and TV viewer along with, I suspect, thousands of other kindred souls, I write to convey my disappointment with the BBC's timing of *Match Of The Day*.

Until the Beeb got its hands on Sunday afternoon football my day was devoted to the pagan ritual of playing football until 12.30, the customary after game analysis at the local watering hole, until closing time (a factor, incidentally, which influenced the timing of Thames' *Big Match* in moving it back from 2.00 to 2.30!). Back home for Sunday lunch and football simultaneously. Followed by ten minutes or so of the Sunday Film, whereupon the events of the day in proving a little too much sent me involuntarily into deep slumber. Unfortunately the 'Sunday Snooze Syndrome' is still with me, and I fear the thousands of other epicurians who today sat through about 5 minutes of Bette Davis and awoke half-way through the football. So exasperated was I, I turned over to watch *The Muppets*, a highly agreeable programme at that time of day, and regret to advise you that I have resolved not to watch BBC TV until *Match Of The Day* is reinstated to its rightful slot at 2.30 p.m.

Two points on Mr Norris's letter. It wasn't the BBC's doing to put their *Match Of The Day* on Sunday but as a result of a compromise following LWT Programme Controller, Michael Grade's attempt to corner

the soccer market.
And it is, of course, LWT who puts out *The Big Match* in the London area and not Thames.
The BBC's soccer coverage has come in for so much buffeting since its shift to Sunday that it's good to be able to print this letter from Simon Jellis of Letchworth, Herts.

> I would like to congratulate the BBC Commentary Team, for excellent football coverage last season. For me they were the best commentary team out of all the Channels. With Jimmy Hill with his good summary of the match, John Motson with his exciting commentary and Barry Davies with his shouts of 'a real beauty' and 'oh! What a goal!'
>
> So far the BBC has carried on where they left off last season, with superb commentary.

One satisfied customer there for soccer, another here for darts. Mrs Sarah Miller of Finchley, London N3, to be precise.

> Dear Barry Took.
>
> The coverage of the darts on BBC2 is up to it's usual high standard. - Smashing! Keep it up!

A letter of appreciation now from Rose Griffiths of Swanage, Dorset, on the subject of snooker.

"May I express my thanks for the enjoyment of the Snooker Championships.

The good manners, elegant appearance, plus the skill of the players, the considerate absorbed audience and the helpful commentators make the programme a real joy."

Mrs C. Frost of Thornaby, Cleveland, wouldn't agree. She writes –

Why don't the BBC organizers of International Snooker ensure that the audience they allow into the theatre is healthy!

Each programme seems to have a large proportion of Bronchitis sufferers, and their ghastly racket must surely put the players off their stroke (or perhaps that's the idea!)

May I suggest an issue of cough Lozenges to the real sufferers and gags for the ones who know their families are listening for them!

And Mrs Alun Evans of Pinner gets quite terse on the subject.

Can you do anything about the BBC televising relays of men wandering around a table with a four foot stick, hitting 22 balls, for hours on end ? I regret that my marriage is being snookered, and in retaliation I would like to make a dreadful curse, 'May all balls be pinched'. I dread this yearly excursion, and would like my share of the TV licence returned.

But now golf – on the whole a popular TV sport, or rather, as one correspondent pointed out, game. Here's Mrs Audrey Francis of South Molton, Devon, on the subject.

Having just watched the exciting final of the Suntory World Matchplay Championships, I would like to congratulate the BBC on the superb coverage – under most difficult conditions.

Added to this, we had the extra bonus of Peter Alliss – his anecdotes, and wealth of information, are as entertaining as the game itself. His comments always kind, funny, impromptu in the inimitable manner that only Peter Alliss can produce.

In fact, Golf without Alliss would be like *Points Of View* without Barry Took. Unthinkable!

I entirely agree! Now, anyone for badminton? Mrs Judith Philpott of Caldicot, Gwent, certainly.

Ahhhh! How badly we badminton fans are treated by the BEEB; I refer of course to Thursday evening's broadcast of The Friends Provident Masters tournament. The allocated time had come to an end and the ladies' singles match was cut – <u>ONE POINT</u> from the final score. I have yet to see a football match cut <u>before</u> 'time', or a horse race before the horses pass the winning post.

I sympathise. Not that I know one end of a shuttlecock from the other, but I can understand enthusiasm, like that of Eric Dunn of Nafferton, East Yorkshire, on the subject of bowls –

The Jack High programme presented by the BBC last week, of the Kodak Masters Bowling Championship was a real treat. Please can we have *more* Flat Green Bowling in your sports programmes. I am sure that I speak for many thousands of bowlers young and old in this our green and pleasant land.

Yours hopefully.

Yes, there's a lot to be said for our green and pleasant land. One of the principal attractions of horse racing has always seemed to me to be the scenery. But not for everyone. Betty Esplin of Arbroath, Angus, wrote to me in September 1980 –

Dear Barry Took, In case you are not aware of it there is a battle going on between Willie Carson and Lester Piggott for the title of Champion Jockey 1980.

Last Saturday things must have really hotted up, for the announcer of the 10 p.m. News had Willie Carson at the Haydock meeting and being placed second to Lester Piggott in the 3.45 p.m. race. Not once did he state this but twice. Mr Carson was in a race at Kempton at 3.30 p.m. and 4 p.m., but if he managed to get to Haydock for the 3.45 p.m. and dash or should I say fly back, then he deserves the title.

Carson duly won the title, so clearly he does have that little something extra.

But from sport we turn to sports commentators . . .

Chapter Eight

THEY ALSO SERVE WHO ONLY STAND AND SHOUT

Our section on sports commentators gets under weigh with this letter from Ian Maccabe, Lieutenant Commander R.N. (retd.), of Dorchester, Dorset.

Comment has been made recently on the extra hazards confronting competitors outside those normally encountered in ther chosen sports, namely the 'commentator handicap', particularly evident in tennis, cricket, snooker, show jumping, darts, golf, etc. E.g.: '. . . batting now with great authority . . .', '. . . well in line now for this year's trophy . . .', '. . . one rather feels that no one can catch him now . . .', and other doom laden pronouncements too numerous to mention.

Now a more subtle and terrifying device to demoralise the sportsmen has emerged. What better way to destroy Aoki and Roger's chances in the Wentworth World Matchplay Championship than to deliver the dreaded Black Spot via the *Radio Times*? (*Radio Times*, 11 October, page 32, col. 3, para 1). Once their names had been advertised as being in the semi-finals on Saturday their chances of getting through the quarter final on the previous day were about nil.

Should we not return to the system whereby BBC sports commentators did just that and left the precarious business of forecasting to those who are used to getting it wrong, the weathermen?

I'm sure Mrs Bobbie Thomas of Grimsby would agree with Mr Maccabe.

Dear Mr Took, Why-oh-why do commentators have to open their *big* mouths?

I refer of course to the ladies doubles badminton (*Grandstand* – Saturday). As soon as the British pair took the lead by *only* one point, Mister Barry Davies had to comment 'dare I say it, but the British girls now have the wind in their sails to win this game.'

And what happens? The usual story – We lose the next three points and of course the game!!

Please tell Mr Davies from me, 'no, you dare *not* say it, just *shut up*.'

Dennis R. Hyde of Liskeard, Cornwall, writes on the subject of top crown bowls.

May I say how much I enjoy the BBC's Top Crown series, especially as it is so easily followed *with the Volume turned down*! Harry Rigby's inane & childish remarks & phrases Completely spoil the programme!

Beatrice Saunders of Weybridge, Surrey, writes on the subject of tennis commentators.

I dislike criticising either the radio or television because there are so many *excellent* programmes. *but* do you think someone would ask the tennis commentators to talk *a little less*. We cannot concentrate on the strokes or the tactics when we are given a lecture between each rally. Surely no one watches tennis who has no knowledge of the game. And, incidentally, everything the commentator says is so obvious.

Beatrice Saunders concludes her letter, which I found a model of restraint, by commenting on the 'blessings' of television and says, of course people criticise it but 'It is only at the tree loaded with fruit that people throw stones.'
Well, if tennis is the tree, here are a couple of stone throwers. First, D. F. Spade of Grays, Essex.

I was today disgusted almost to the point of physical illness by hearing the tennis commentator John Barrett declare that John McEnroe has "an over-developed sense of justice and fair play". Such a sense must surely be the very last thing which would motivate this lout, whom many of us find quite nauseating enough without being told that his boorishness is, in reality, evidence of moral rectitude. Does the BBC really want to convey to its viewers - many of whom are young and impressionable - that such behaviour is not only acceptable but desirable, and if not, do we really need the consistently inane Mr. Barrett?

Next, Pamela Moffat of Guildford.

'Dear Barry Took, isn't it high time that Dan Maskell was superannuated. His illuminating glimpses of the obvious and his running tallies of Aces, Double Faults, etc., are a pain in the neck. I am numerate and have no need of these aids. You may say why not cut out the sound to which I would reply that one cannot appreciate tennis to the full on TV without hearing the sound of ball on gut, along with the exchanges of various competitors with umpires and crowd.'

A point well made, if a trifle didactic.
Well, sports commentators are a tough breed. At least I hope they are. I can't bear the thought of all those tear-stained pillows as they

sob themselves to sleep after the harsh remarks of their viewers. If you're a connoisseur of harsh words, consider this letter from M. Hodgkinson of Dartford in Kent (how appropriate) on the subject of Darts.

> I am compelled to write to complain about the staggering hopelessness of the commentators for the darts this Tuesday. Their counting is bad; six obvious mistakes were made on the late coverage Tuesday. An innocent Belgian Luc Mareel was in the space of two games called Lucky Mareel, Locky Mareel, Luck, Look, Luke and at one point Lofty! Mr Green observed "I don't know what he said but it was in Belgian" – what? Mr Waddel described him as a "Macbeth like character" and followed by saying that he, (Mareel) would be très heureux (pronounced tres huru) "if this goes in" – Indeed!
>
> Mr Waddel noticed his "lack of beer-gut" and said it was "a credit to the game".
>
> The image of darts to the public of being a beer drinkers domain is being influenced less by the size of participants stomachs, than by the inarticulate, innumerate, pretentious banality of its commentary.

But enough of abuse. Here's a little praise for that prince of anchormen, Frank Bough. It comes from B. Cooper of Sheffield.

> I wonder how many people share my view of Frank Bough? He is without doubt a most professional and likeable man. I have always admired his stylish equanimity

I share your view, Mr Cooper. More praise from Bill Hudson of Penrith.

"Dear Barry Took, I think all racing commentators should go for lessons to Peter O'Sullevan.

In my opinion he stands out a mile in this field – a real masterpiece."

Anne Pettitt writes from Dublin suggesting a sports commentator's award, and says –

"My vote would go to Peter Alliss for his excellent coverage of the golf. He is a joy to listen to and his little comments about each player are delightful. He is never rude but when a competitor plays a bad shot he just says 'what a dreadful shot' or 'not very well played sir' and he is just wonderful. I could listen to him all day. My second choice would go to Dan Maskell for the tennis. He only says the bare minimum and yet is most informative."

A nice one for Dan Maskell there – and here, from Barry Harlow of New Addington, Croydon, Surrey, is a tribute to John Arlott.

I am bringing up the subject of commentators again, but this time to thank one in particular. John Arlott has brought me endless pleasure commentating on cricket on television and radio.

I am sure that other cricket fans will join me in thanking John for his superb commentary and in wishing him many happy years in retirement.

Finally, in this section, a letter that is unsigned. All I know is that it comes from Ramsgate. Its message is clear and to the point.

I am fed up with tese selfish people who keep moaning about the sports commentators. I am blind and without them I would not be able to follow the many sports I enjoy! Like most blidn people I like to lead a normal life, and prefer watching T.V. with my family than shutting myself away in another room just because I can't follow what is going on. Well done.

Chapter Nine

NEWSPEOPLE

Anyone who sits regularly in front of the cameras is bound to attract a great deal of attention and this is more true of newsreaders than any other television personality. Many newsreaders have become a national institution, and the viewers love them or hate them; criticise their clothes, their posture, their height, their hair. One thing about being a newsreader – you're never ignored. Mrs Winifred Symonds of Bournemouth, expresses herself thus on the subject.

> I like all the BBC News readers, as I think they are all very gentlemanly and immaculate. I also like Jan Leeming very much. She reads the News alone and has a pleasing personality and a charming smile. I much prefer the BBC to the ITV.

Mrs Symonds also comments –

> I was delighted to see John Edmunds back again. I saw him for the first time fifteen years ago and he hasn't changed a bit: just as handsome.

And Miss K. Kennedy of Lewisham, S.E.13, feels much the same way.

> What a joy it is to have John Edmunds on the news again. Not only is he a pleasure to listen to, but also a pleasure to look at. As the news itself is mostly depressing such a charming personality goes some way towards lightening the burden.

Every idiosyncrasy of everyone who appears on the news is noted by our correspondents. Joan Baker of Beccles, Suffolk, wrote to me last November commenting on Brian Curtois.

As always he was concise and clear in his account, *but* once again he appeared to be gazing at the heavens the while. No one else has their prompt board in such an elevated position, and we are so distracted by it that I am at last driven to write and ask if anyone else has noticed it?

Perhaps he's looking for divine guidance.

Mrs Rosamund Smith of Doncaster asks –

Could you please tell me if Martin Adeny is in training to row the Atlantic Ocean? We find his arm movements most frustrating, and cannot concentrate on the news he reads for counting his arm excercises.
If he cannot control this, would some one *please* give him something to hold.

Someone signing himself C. L. H. of Callington, Cornwall, asks apropos Kenneth Kendall –

Would somebody please provide Keneth Kendal with a cushion? It seems that many times during the Nine O'Clock News, he is trying to edge himself up on his seat by use of his elbows.
Has somebody polished his seat or is he really that short?

Actually, Kenneth is slightly above average height, and I tend to agree with Zoe Graham of Old Woodstock, who wrote to me in September 1980 –

> I think Kenneth Kendell is really very nice, and he reads the news very well, I thought I must congratulate the BBC1 for choosing such a nice, kind, happy man.

Richard Baker is, of course, much loved by one and all, and when he returns from leave we always receive a flutter of mail – these two comments being typical. The first is from Stella Cook of Clevedon, Avon. The second is from Chris Pendlebury of Birmingham.

> We are delighted to see that Richard Baker is back again to the read the news.

> I'm so pleased that last week Richard Baker and this week the judicious and ubiquitous Angela Rippon have again given the news on BBC-1 and BBC-2. If only the news could always be read by one of these two, Kenneth Kendall or Jan Leeming, the news would always sound good, even when it was not. I prefer them to other news-readers, who in contrast with them cannot make the news sound good, even when it is.

I like the description of Angela Rippon as 'judicious and ubiquitous'. I guess Mrs P. A. Wakeford of Wraysbury, Berks, would agree. She says –

> How wonderful to have Miss Angela Rippon back. She is absolutely beautiful to look at and her voice is

a joy to listen to. Also she is so natural and completely unaffected that I hope, if she ever has to go she will train any who have to follow her.

As we all now know, Miss Rippon will be quitting the BBC in the not too distant future to join the new commercial breakfast TV set-up. The next two letters seem to suggest that she's already been preparing for the change. Ivor Hitchings of Newark, Notts., wrote last November –

Dear Mr Took, After your programme this evening – I noticed Angela Rippon was reading the News in my wife's old dressing gown. Did she go to our local jumble sale?

And of the same occasion, Mrs Jean Daly of Ealing commented

Had Angela Rippon had a bath and got ready for bed before she read the nine o'clock news this evening? Her dressing-gown was similar to mine although a different colour.

One last word on Miss Rippon from J. L. Hartley of Derby –

Can it be that Angela Rippon uses Super Glue to prevent movement of her eyebrows?

For every letter we've received on *Points Of View* about Angela Rippon we've received a dozen about Jan Leeming, who became a regular news reader in 1980. In September, Judy Burns, of Theydon Bois, commented –

After watching your programme last week, I was amazed to see Jan Leeming appear to read the nine o'clock news in her dressing gown!

Ah – the old dressing gown again. The poor girl came in for a lot of criticism about her appearance. M. B. Cummings of Abingdon, Oxon, wrote to say –

Whilst I appreciate that the BBC have found it necessary during these difficult times to make drastic spending cuts one would have thought that enough money could have been found to supply Jan Leeming with more than one jumper.

One of many on the same subject – but 'unfair' cried John Law of Sandbank, Dunoon.

How dare some viewers criticise Miss Jan Leeming's dress! She has no airs or graces and is the perfect News Reader. She doesn't try to put over her personal opinions like some I know by using inflections of the voice. Her elfin looks enchant us at the above address. So tell these carpers to belt up!

Barbara Marshall of Birkdale, Southport, likes the way Jan Leeming looks, and asks . . .

Would you kindly ask the lovely Jan Leeming to stand up after reading the news.
Reason So we can have a nifty look at her outfits. I know it's not practical but at least it would cheer us all up after crying all the way through the programme.

And the last word on the subject of Miss Leeming goes to Brian Kewell of Canterbury who wrote –

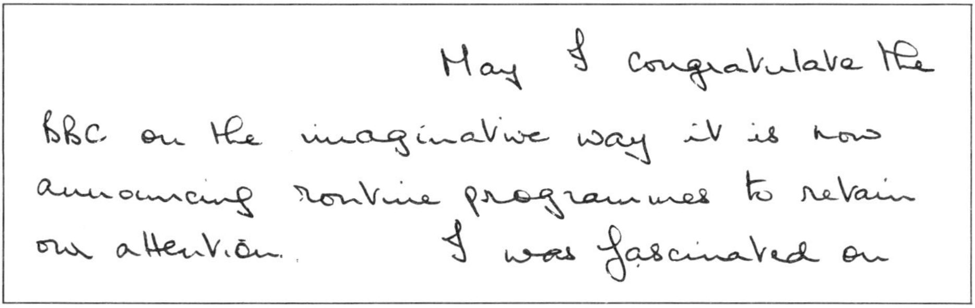
May I congratulate the BBC on the imaginative way it is now announcing routine programmes to retain our attention. I was fascinated on

Saturday evening to hear that the next programme would be the News .... and Sport with Jan Leeming! Slow Motion or Action Replay!

Finally, on the subject of newsreaders we received this letter from Jean Cox of Bicester.

Watching the *serious* newsreaders, carefully and *seriously* gathering up the news sheets at the end of each News programme, I long for the day when one of them – perhaps that *most serious* of all newsreaders, Richard Baker – hurls the whole lot up in the air and *seriously* screams!!!!

Chapter Ten

SOME POINTS FROM YOUR LETTERS

In this section of the book I've assembled a group of letters that don't really fit into any particular category, but which caught my eye and demonstrate the wide range of topics about which people write to me. First, a letter from Tamzin Later of Ilford, Essex.

Why does *Nationwide* insist on showing revolting pictures and films, when most people are having their evening meal? Today (17 October) we had delightful scenes of worms, maggots and fleas. I was fortunate enough to be merely eating chips, but I pity anyone who was eating spaghetti!

Next, one in the eye for me from Rodney Day of Margate, Kent.

Dear Barry, I have just heard you state that *The Sky At Night* is to be 'repeated earlier'. Is this a BBC plot to show the repeats before the first showing of programmes?

Yes, well what I meant was . . . come to think of it I'm not sure *what* I meant. Now, here's a letter from Barry Markham of Rugby.

In the debate on currency, I should like to take issue with all those pedants who insist that we should use the word '*pence*'.

After all, if we measure gold in carrots, why shouldn't we measure money in peas?

Loud groans all round.
And here's the observant Michael Paine of Exmouth.

Dear Barry Took, Can you please explain to me why it is that television techniques have advanced to the point that we can bounce a signal off a satellite with ease, but not allow an actor to go upstairs on a set without wobbling the bannisters?

If you don't believe me, look at the *Terry and June* show that preceded your spot last Friday.

Eryl Wyn Williams of Anglesey wrote to me in November 1980 in both English and Welsh.

Why does such a brilliant Programme like 'Small World', BBC 2, have only 10 minutes per week? Surley this is an insult to everyone concerned wilt the programme.

The fantastic sequence of the automoton archer actualy ~~firing~~ shooting an arrow just cries out to be shown again. Please.

Pam mae rhaglen ardderchog fel 'Small World' B.B.C. 2 yn cael ond deg munud yr wythnos? Mae amser fer fel hyn yn sarhad i bawb syn cynhyrchu'r rhaglen.

Yn arbennig, mae darn y fodel saethwr syn saethu saeth yn werth ei weld unwaith eto, os gwelwch yn dda.

Here's another groans all round letter from J. Herbert of East Sutton, Kent.

Crime plays where we are left in the air, wondering whether the Police achieved their objective, are really frustrating. I refer to Juliet Bravo 25 October.

Did the lady get her false leg back? – Or was she left out on a limb?

Talking of groans, J. D. Beause of Chingford, London E.4., writes to me as follows –

Please enlighten me about those picture-less excerpts in news bulletins from the House of Commons!

When we hear those long, loud groaning noises from MP's in the background, are they agreeing, disagreeing or just waking up?

Our elected representatives at work, which brings me to this letter from Linda Morton of Glasgow –

Dear Barry Took
TELL Margret thachter
to stop wavin her
arms about.

On a different subject entirely we received this letter from John P. Sharman of Littlethorpe, Nr Ripon.

Often I hear on both BBC television and BBC radio the mentioning of the third world. Now as I know personally of only one world I would certainly like to know where the third one is, but more importantly what the hell happened to the second one?

Mr Sharman, I'm as puzzled as you are.

J. Moore of Carshalton makes a valid point when he writes –

My point of view is that there is *no* point, *no* logic, in the way that the BBC (mainly on Tuesdays) *ends* one programme on 2 at 9.30 p.m., whilst *starting* another on 1 at 9.25. This means, of course, that if one wishes to watch *both* programmes it is necessary either to switch over from 2 at 9.25 and thus miss the last five minutes of the programme; or, watch it through, and miss the first five minutes of the programme on 1.

I have written to the programme controllers, etc., on more than one occasion complaining of this total lack of logic, but always get a stock printed reply, to the effect that 'The BBC receives many letters, and your comment has been noted . . .' Perhaps you can think of something more helpful to say.

I only wish I could. All I can say is that it does happen and can be irritating. As I've said before, *Points Of View* has been criticised on occasion for being trivial. The trouble is that in a ten-minute programme a serious subject cannot be dealt with in depth. A good example is *The War Game*, the controversial film about nuclear attack, which was made by the BBC but not shown. I print two letters in full on the subject. The first comes from D. Slinger of Gloucester.

> 'When are violence and 'horror' acceptable viewing? Answer: When they are neatly packaged with sexual deviations as pure voyeuristic entertainment. Example: Monday's film *An Investigation of Murder* about the actions and life style of a deviant mass murderer.
>
> When are violence and horror not acceptable? Answer: When they are part of a serious presentation of the most vital question facing humanity. Example: *The War Game*, made by the BBC in 1965 but denied a showing ever since. Reason: The BBC knows what the establishment knows is good for us.'

The second comes from Colin Livesey of Manchester.

I would like to ask you why the B.B.C has, as yet, declined to broadcast the film 'The War Game', as I feel that the people of the U.K. have the right to see this, particularly in view of the Deployment of Cruise missiles and overall increase in Nuclear weapons in Britain. I note that the B.B.C. has already screened other programmes concerning both Nuclear war and it's aftermath and even Biological/Chemical warfare which is not supposed to exist!

Please do answer this as I know that a great many people would like this film to be screened so as to give the public the information they should have. I am not an alarmist but just a realist and I recognise that many people do not or will not recognise the indescribeable horrors which a Nuclear attack shall bring upon this country.

Many of our correspondents are deeply committed Christians and feel a perfectly understandable sense of outrage when their beliefs are attacked. Here's Mrs Meg Lovett of Morecambe on the subject of *Not The Nine O'Clock News.*

Last week I switched on to the *Not The Nine O'Clock News* programme. Quite by accident I can assure you. I immediately heard four people give a parody on our Christian Creed and our Advocate Jesus Christ.

Oh it was clever, it was even funny, I think the Lord himself would have a quiet chuckle (we have no right to assume he doesn't have a sense of humour, the laugh is on us, he made us male and female), but oh in what appalling taste.

It must have been very offensive to the millions of people in the world who respect our Christian faith. Come on Christians, where are you, stand up and be counted, are we going to allow this without a protest.

We Christians who know our Lord Jesus Christ and love him didn't think it was funny, just sick. Tell them please.

I can assure Mrs Lovett that she was not alone in her protest. Hundreds wrote in the same vein. The strange thing about *Not The Nine O'Clock News* is that it splits the audience in two – the young love it, the not so young abhor it. Susan L. Denwood of Cliriger, Nr. Burnley in Lancashire, spoke for the former group when she wrote to me last December to express her feelings about –

that *brilliant, witty* and *superb* programme – *Not The Nine O'Clock News.*

The 'Fab Four', Rowan, Griff, Mel and Pamela are really the tops!

They will do another series – won't they??? If not, I for one will return to complete and utter sanity – how boring!

Michael Parkinson, or his guests anyway, rouse equally vivid For or Against reactions. Here's Mrs E. McLellan of Paisley on the subject of Billy Connolly.

Billy Connolly must be one of the most offensive 'entertainers' on TV. Any humour he possesses is negated by his crudity. Why Michael Parkinson persists in asking him back, I do not understand.

To place Barbara Woodhouse and Angie Dickinson in the position of having to politely applaud such coarseness must have been a great embarrassment to both ladies.

And here is Mrs J. Cliffe of Bradford writing about Brian Clough.

Three cheers for Brian Clough. Previous to hearing him being interviewed on the Mike Parkinson show on Wednesday 12 November I had always considered him rather a brash person. However he soared in my estimation when he asked a celebrity to be careful of her language because his children were watching the programme. There must be thousands of people in this country who object to the foul language used on television.

And, of course, there *are* thousands, most of whom write to me. Michael Parkinson has many admirers and, it goes without saying, his detractors too. When the news of Mike's Australian deal was announced, Mr I. R. Francis of Hanworth, Middlesex, sat down and wrote this –

I am not in the least surprised that someone should think it worth £1,000,000 to send Michael Parkinson to Australia for 3 years, but I am astonished that it is Australian rather than British money, and disappointed that it is only for 6 months of each year.

Could you start an appeal for a further £1,000,000 to make it full time, and preferably permanent? If so I will start it off with £10.

Any chat show is as good as its guests, and when they're of the calibre of Arthur Marshall it produces this sort of reaction from Mrs D. Eckersley of Cheadle, Cheshire.

How I laughed at Arthur Marshall on last night's *Michael Parkinson Show* – a truly funny man! I have enjoyed his humour since his early radio impersonations of a girls' school mistress in charge of the 'croc', but on Saturday he surpassed himself.

My thanks to him for the best laugh in months!

And on that cheery note, we move on.

Chapter Eleven

PROS AND CONS

I wrote in my introduction about the 'tidal effect' of letters for and against a programme. In this section I'd like to illustrate this by reprinting what has been said for and against some comedy and drama productions. First, the almost universally popular *Butterflies*.
Miss S. Graves of Hertford writes –

> What a marvellous series *Butterflies* has been this time around. Carla Lane has really excelled herself this time. Well done Carla! and what great acting by all the cast.

But James Morris of Cheltenham feels differently.

> ‘I would just like to say how disappointing I've found the new series of *Butterflies*. Not only has the subject matter been in very poor taste, but also has become far too serious and has therefore spoilt much of the enjoyment that was present in the previous series.
>
> As we live in Cheltenham, where it was filmed, we were all extremely interested in what *was* a good family comedy, but now it is just an embarrassment.’

While we're on the subject of *Butterflies*, I enjoyed receiving this letter from Mrs B. Addis of Harrogate.

> I too have enjoyed *Butterflies* but must confess to grave misgivings about the paternity of one of Ria's sons. For is it not true that two straight haired parents cannot have a curly haired child? Ria's relations with the 'other man', I fear, have not always been on quite such a spiritual level as they are now depicted! !!

I say, look here, Mrs Addis, what *are* you suggesting? I suppose that *A Tale Of Two Cities* is as far removed from *Butterflies* as you can imagine. The BBC's recent adaptation produced a strong reaction from our correspondents. Suzanne Dobson of Calne, Wiltshire, loved it.

Having just finished watching the last episode of Dickens' *Tale Of Two Cities* I feel it my duty to congratulate the BBC. It was superb!

Paul Shelley portrayed both Carton and Darney equally well and, in my opinion, Dickens would have been proud to see his novel acted with such feeling.

Roy Coulthard of London E.6., on the other hand, had grave misgivings.

I felt compelled to write in protest regarding the explicit 'nightmare' sequence shown in last night's showing of the new Sunday serial, *A Tale Of Two Cities*.

My family were eagerly awaiting the start of the programme when we were met with unnecessarily gory shots of a guillotine falling and blood spilling to be soaked up by some material. All very clever I thought but not the sort of thing one associates with early evening viewing. Nevertheless we stuck with it, then the nightmare sequence began. I glanced across at my 8½-year-old son who was absolutely petrified. I must say I felt quite uneasy about it myself and at that point turned the television off.

I fail to see why the scene should have been made in such a way to disturb young minds.

It seems to me that these 'shock' scenes should be confined to X certificate films not to peak hour television programmes.

This is the first time in my life that I have written in this way as I have always believed that if anything on TV offends, it can always be switched off, which I did in this instance, but unfortunately the harm was already done.

We had many letters in the same vein, although, as I say, on the whole the series was well-liked. We received many letters on the subject of The Play For Today, *C_2H_5OH.* I reprint one from Mrs Doreen Thompson of Newcastle upon Tyne.

> BRILLIANT, that is the only word in the english language adequate to describe Dinsdale Landen's interpretation of an alcoholic in "C2H5OH" I was spellbound from start to finish. I sincerely hope that when the T.V. awards are handed out that Dinsdale Landen is at the top of the list for this "Gem" of a performance.
> Well done Dinsdale, and Thankyou.

But we also received this letter from D. T. Allsop of the Scottish Council on Alcoholism, which I reproduce in full.

> We would like to comment on the recent play "C_2H_5Oh". The treatment of a very real problem was, in our opinion, extremely shallow and almost so artificial as to bring into question whether the whole play was intended to be serious or humorous.
>
> The quite ridiculous relationship which developed between the principal actor and the doctor, the so called counselling session ("you can always get married again"), coupled with the almost manic behaviour of the other residents could, together, have the effect of putting many people off attending for in-patient treatment at an alcoholism treatment unit. These factors, coupled with the undue emphasis placed on fits when withdrawing from tranquillising drugs, present a far from accurate picture of a "drying-out" process.
>
> This play, together with the farcical film "The Cracker Factory" shown the previous week, have focused a lot of viewing time on alcohol problems very recently. Whilst such attention is, in general, very welcome, we suggest that it might be worthy of consideration that specialist agencies should be approached for their advice on programme content, rather than screen uninformed and potentially dangerous nonsense.

The screen version of *Dr Jekyll and Mr Hyde* produced a telegram (!) from D. Logan of Leicester.

> CONGRATULATIONS BBC 2 DR JEKYLL MR HYDE LEFT ME SCARED TO LOOK IN MIRROR ''JUST PLAIN TERRYFINGLY TERRIFIC''
> D LOGAN 9 FROME AVENUE OADBY LEICESTER

And shortly after, this letter from Geoffrey Tier of Chorleywood, Herts.

Dear Barry Took, Yesterday evening (Thursday November 20th) we were watching *Dr Jekyll and Mr Hyde* when I turned to my wife and asked her: 'Where's that funny *whirring* noise coming from?' 'Oh,' she replied, 'that's only R. L. Stevenson turning in his grave.'

All honour to David Hemmings for doing what he could, but not even the most skilful workman can produce a masterpiece without proper tools, and one can neither make a silk purse out of a sow's ear nor a credible piece of television out of a warped rehash of a great novel.

It's said that 'it's a difference of opinion that makes horse racing', and the same can also be said of drama, as here in the case of *The Happy Autumn Fields*. First a letter from Jacquie Seddon of Welling, Kent.

> I would like to say how much I enjoyed the BBC 2 Playhouse 'The Happy Autumn Fields'.
>
> The landscapes shown of the golden summer fields contrasted beautifully with the Edwardian claustrophobic interiors of the house.
>
> It then shows how much times have changed from beauty to mechanical disaster.
>
> Henrietta and Sarah who were the two sisters were wonderfully portrayed by Tracy Childs and Felicity Dean.

But Miss N. Brinkley of Ashford Common, Middlesex, asks:

I wonder if I am alone in finding it so difficult to see some of the plays, conducted in almost total darkness.

I have learnt to follow the action by recognising two round sparkling things as eyes, and a white round thing as a man's collar.

I know *some* of the action has to be presented thus, but not *all*.

I have just seen *The Happy Autumn Fields*. The scene in the drawing room had maids carrying lamps, so it was obviously *meant* to be lighted, but I only saw maids' uniforms, and guessed that there were figures in the background.

Then I saw through the gloom an interesting piece of scenery, two hills and a tower, but after a few minutes it moved, and I found it was a lady's face.

I find this all most disconcerting.

The one play of recent months to receive universal praise was *Caught On A Train* and as there aren't any 'antis', here are some of the 'pros'. First, Mrs G. Harris of Newcastle upon Tyne.

I have just finished watching what I consider to be the finest play shown on television this year. I refer of course to the excellent *Caught On A Train*, which literally brimmed over with fine acting and kept me thoroughly engrossed for its entire one hour twenty minutes running time.

I offer my congratulations to Dame Peggy Ashcroft and Michael Kitchen for their superb performances and indeed to the entire production team of this marvellous production.

Keep up the good work Beeb.

And finally, I quote one line from Mr E. A. Holder of Reading's letter on the subject.

PLAYHOUSE : CAUGHT ON A TRAIN

TELEVISION HAS ATTAINED PERFECTION.

Chapter Twelve

TO THE MANOR BORN

An almost universal favourite with viewers has been *To The Manor Born*, and the thing that has struck me as I've read letter after letter on the subject is the chatty approach of most correspondents. This is, of course, mainly because of the warmth of that super comedy actress, Penelope Keith. As Mrs Lily E. Rubbathan of Crewe says –

> Dear Barry, *To The Manor Born* is a half hour of rib-tickling fun. Please ask Penelope to stay as 'bitter-sweet' as she is. She's delightful.

And here's what Mrs P. A. Gow of Stevenage, Herts, has to say on the subject of *To The Manor Born*.

> I enjoy it immensely and think it is superbly witty and sarcastic, beautifully portrayed by all the actors.
>
> So many people have been, shall we say 'deflated' financially these days, but I wonder how many in real life would take it in their stride as well as our 'Audrey'.

But, Edward M. Buxton, of Loughborough, has a complaint.

> Shame on you all at the BBC.
>
> You had us all on tenterhooks waiting to hear Audrey's nickname last Sunday, and you never told us.
>
> But I forgive you because *To The Manor Born* is great, and long may it reign.

Kate Ashbrook of Exeter makes this comment on the programme –

'To the Manor Born' seems to contain some glaring inaccuracies. In the last series we were told that Aud and Marj were Benenden Old Girls. Yet in a recent programme we were shown their school magazine and it was quite different from the Benenden mag I received this year, last year or any other year. The school photo looked wrong too. And, incidentally, Benenden Old Girls are not called Old Girls but Seniors.

Personally, I don't think Aud or Marj have ever been near Benenden. But I wish they had!

This next letter clouds the issue still further. It comes from Lyn Needham of Rickmansworth.

> I have just been watching *To The Manor Born* and was very surprised to see Penelope Keith referring to one of my old school magazines as her old school's magazine. Did she actually go to Haberdashers Aske's School for Girls or was it just an old magazine belonging to someone behind the scenes?

Perhaps we will never know. Another mystery surrounds the signature tune – we received many letters about it. This, from Caroline Wilson of York, is fairly typical.

Is my imagination playing tricks with me or is the BBC using the same theme tune for "To the Manor Born" as for "Yes, Minister"?

Is this the latest move in the BBC's economy drive? What will be next? Using the theme tune of "Blankety Blank" for "Mastermind"?

And on the subject of economy, Katie Rock, of Twickenham, writes –

I was shocked on Sunday, when I turned on the television to watch *To The Manor Born* to see Penelope Keith without (dare I say it) a bra on. Is this one of the BBC's cut backs, or is it a boob!

Jessica Callard, aged 9, of Neath, has noticed something else –

Dear Barry Took, I know that Mrs Audrey fforbes Hamilton is not as rich as she used to be, but surely even she can afford a few more pairs of shoes.

Nearly every week in *To The Manor Born* she seems to wear the same pair of brown shoes. My mother has got a pair just like them and she says that they are very comfortable – perhaps this is the explanation.

Doubtless it is, Jessica. It's amazing what viewers notice.

Tom E. Chilton of Brighton wrote to tell me –

Mr de Vere certainly deserves an award in the next honours list for his admirable self sacrifice in looking after tenants' property on his estate.

Almost a month ago he engaged a man to see that this work was carried out. As we haven't seen the poor chap since, he must be worked to a frazzle. And yet, since the series first began, exterior shots of Grantly Manor illustrate its desperate need for a coat of paint. I am sure it is only the ivy holding the place up.

I have a suspicion that I may be partly to blame for this epidemic of 'eagle eye' among viewers. Mrs Beryl Murray of Dartford, Kent, says –

Since your programme has appeared on Television, I find I am more observant than I used to be.

Take "To the Manor Born" – how come Penelope Keith was charged £1.00, by the 'happy' Post mistress, for a basketful of Goodies, & when She was unpacking them, I counted 4 Bananas, several apples, (which were selected from the front) & Some tins with unknown contents.
If I could purchase so many items for £1.00, I would change my retailer, & put up with her "cheerful" manner".

Here's Stan Kent of Sheffield on the same matter –

In *To The Manor Born* on 26 October, we saw Audrey fforbes Hamilton visit the village shop and buy *potatoes, apples* and *bananas*. When she arrived home we saw her unpacking TINS. I've heard of Water into Wine, but *spuds* into *cans*?

And, of course, as we all know everybody spots lapses in continuity. Here are two letters on the subject of the Grantly Manor weather. The first is from John Bell of Carisbrooke, Isle of Wight.

In last Sunday's episode of *To The Manor Born*, Marjorie was seen walking to the cottage on a bright sunny day. When she arrived there, the view through the window showed the countryside covered in snow!

Either the lane is a long way from the cottage, and it took Marjorie about eight months to reach it, or the location for the series is centred around an area of very unpredictable weather.

And in Llanfairpwll, Ceri and Sian Owen noticed the same amazing effect.

How it must have snowed at Grantly Manor last week.

As Marjorie came up the drive to the lodge wheeling her bicycle amidst rural greenery, little did she imagine the blizzard that would rage twixt front door and drawing room. Inches of snow had blanched the rural scene to be viewed through the windows.

But continuity lapses or not, the programme is still much enjoyed, certainly by Jeanette Cave, aged 11, of Leicester.

I think that "To The Manor Born" is an absolutely super programme. All the actors in it are wonderful, including Ole Ned.

But there are dissenting voices. Edward G. Thompson of Gloucester finds one aspect of the series distasteful.

Being in private service as Butler etc., for forty years I found the part played by the Butler (*To The Manor Born*) *disgusting antics* to a Highly Honoured worthwhile profession.

And Julia Hunt of Smallfield, Nr Horley, Surrey, writes –

Am I the only *one* who hates *To The Manor Born*?

Clearly not, Julia. Mrs M. Carnie of Bath shares your view.

I can't stand that woman in *To The Manor Born*. She is too much like Margaret Thatcher and one Thatcher is one too many. Class distinction is a disease and not a subject to be treated lightly. Get rid of the programme and Penelope Keith. She's about as funny as Joe Stalin.

PS My husband bets me you won't dare show this letter, it might ruin your chances in the honours list.

Your husband loses the bet, Mrs Carnie! But frankly, I consider my chance of making the honours list is so slight as to be not worth considering. After all, if they could overlook Daley Thompson . . . But let's not dwell on such things, and end with this note from Ruth MacDonald of Dun Laoire, Eire.

> I am very pleased to see that *To The Manor Born* is back on the BBC. I think Penelope Keith is one of the funniest ladies around.

A sentiment with which I entirely agree.

Chapter Thirteen

TRIANGLE

The three hundred letters or so that we received on the subject of the serial *Triangle* could make a book on their own. Surprisingly, opinions were fairly equally divided and I reprint a representative selection here. R. M. Foote of Cambridge wrote on 25 March 1981 –

> 'Triangle' is so awful it is compulsive viewing in my family.
>
> Today the engineer fell down the stairs and hit the back of his head but ended up with plaster on his forehead!
>
> I can't wait for the next episode!

Stephen Murray of Brampton, Cumbria (he assures me he's *not* the distinguished actor!), wrote on the same day in a similar vein –

> Dear Mr Took, *Triangle* . . . Is this absurd play worthy of the Guinness Book of Records for fatuity? This ill-conducted ship is engaged on a voyage which, I would think, would not justify a ship of that sort; she is permanently in calm water, which seems unlikely; and (less surprisingly) there are almost no passengers.

However, the play has the advantage that it unglues one from the TV, so making time for doing something useful instead.

And here's E. Murdoch of Bradford.

As a mere man who has to sit through a great deal of rubbish on TV or go out and dig the garden, I was pleased to say 'Goodbye' to that doleful serial called *Angels*, where twice a week neurotic so-called nurses argued, wept and screamed abuse at each other till we the viewers dreaded the thoughts of ever being ill enough to go to hospital.

In its place however we are now offered the delights of a cruise liner on its triangular trips to Felixstowe, Gothenberg and Amsterdam. But not for us viewers the delights of scenes ashore in Amsterdam or Gothenberg etc. and why? Because the boat is run by a similar arguing, backbiting, spying, drunken, neurotic, suicidal, ex criminal bunch, like the staff of St Angela's.

We are now worried about ever taking a cruise anywhere.

But now a couple of 'fors' typical of many. The first came from Caroline Richardson of Coventry.

I would like to compliment the BBC on that marvellous series 'Triangle'. I find it great and live for Mondays and Wednesdays.

I think that Kate O'Hara and Larry Lamb's portrayals as their respective characters are marvellous.

And Lisa James of Pontyclun, Mid Glamorgan, would seem to agree. She wrote –

I am writing to defend the marvellous new series 'Triangle'. Its very interesting and the acting of Larry Lamb, Michael Craig, Kate O'Mara and others is splendid. I hope it continues into many series.

But back to the dissenting voices. Here's Mr B. F. Watts of Norwich

Dear Barry, About that dreadful series *Triangle*, both my wife and I think it's the most boring thing the BBC have put on the tele for years. This programme has about as much life as a deceased parrot and much less colour.

Don Kling of Crawley, Sussex, wrote *this* on Friday, 13 March.

Dear Barry Took, It remains a constant source of amazement to me that the good ship in the series *Triangle* manages to remain afloat, both physically and financially! At full speed, day and night, the ship navigates the busy shipping lanes of the North Sea without a soul on the bridge, but does it really matter as the ship does not carry any passengers and only one car, belonging to you know who.

I feel a more apt name for this stupid series would be . . . no I am unable to think of a name that you could repeat on your very fine programme. If we are lucky enough, maybe the crew will kill themselves off and then we could call the series 'The Marie Celeste'.

There were many suggestions as to how the series should end, of varying degrees of rudeness. Typical was this brief note from R. Wood of Bridlington.

> Reference the programme *Triangle* – I suppose one could hope that a 'U' boat could appear or a floating mine and so solve all the problems.

But, as I have said, there were a number of our correspondents who spoke up for the series and as it regularly clocked up an audience of nine million it clearly was compulsive viewing for many, but to be frank it attracted much criticism, much of which was quoted on *Points Of View*, and resulted in our receiving this letter from J. Hallett of Basing, Hants –

> I am repeatedly disgusted and appalled by the shocking reports which continually receive airplay on *Points Of View* concerning the serial *Triangle*.
>
> I have never seen the programme but I am upset that the BBC show such degrading filth in the early hours of the evening. Adult viewing of this calibre should be shown only after 9.00 by which time I have usually finished my homework and am able to watch it.

And on that note, we move on.

Chapter Fourteen

MAINLY ME

As I indicated in the introduction to this book, I get a vast number of letters addressed to me and which are concerned not only with the programme but also with me personally. If the prospect of a short ego trip bores you, stop reading *now*. But who wouldn't be delighted to receive this letter from Isabel Gregory of Crickhowell, Powys.

> My 9 month old sister Kate was so fasenated by you Tonight that every time you appeared she crawled over to TV set ~~and~~ climbed up and kissed you. My brother and I love your programme and Kate seems to love you..

As a counterbalance to that, I received *this* –

> You make me sick with your un-witty comments and your stupid remarks.
> Why don't you leave the BBC altogether?
> As some people would put it, it is utter drivvel.

I get asked a lot of daft questions but none dafter than this from Angus Mackechnie.

> Could we have a close up of your left ear to settle a family argument: my mum says it is pierced but I

think it's not. And my dad says you haven't even got a left ear. Please settle our argument. Thank you Mr Took and say hello to Belinda – my cat.

All I can say to that is I do have a left ear, it isn't pierced, and hello Belinda.

A Mrs Knowles of Northampton asks –

Barry, how do you pronounce your name?
Is it Took as in look or
Is it Took as in wool?

Coming as I do from London I'd have said *both*. Many northerners think of it as in Tuck or Duck and southerners often pronounce it to rhyme with snooker. It's an odd name but surprisingly common. Mary Goodwin of Coventry wrote to me recently saying 'my friend and I think you must be a former school colleague of ours and we wonder if you could set our minds at rest!' The answer to that is no, I'm afraid I wasn't a school colleague of yours. Rachel Goutorbe of Matlock wondered 'if you are a relation of mine . . . My mother is called Dawn Tooke and her sister is called Janet Tooke. Have you dropped the E off Tooke?' Again, the answer is no. I'm afraid we're not related and I've never had an E on the end of my surname. Rhianon Jones, aged 9, of Reynoldstown, Gower, wrote to me

During the war my Grandma had a small boy to stay for a short time in Lampeter. Was that little boy you? because he was called Barry Took and his father was a Royal Marine sergent and it is an unusual name.

Sorry – no relation. Ex Corporal Bottley of KRR's now living in Edenbridge, Kent, wrote to me thus –

Dear Barry, This letter has nothing to do with your TV programme. But can you tell me if you are the son of Edward Took who served with the KRR's in the last war. Billeted at one time at Henley on Thames: I myself was there, and since then I have never come across the name of Took.

The answer is no. My father was Charles William Took and he served in the Royal Navy in World War 1.

In fact, I think I can say to all who have written on the same subject – I'm afraid we're not related, I'm not your old wartime buddy and have never lived in Watford, Portsmouth, Nuneaton, Saxmundham, Manchester, Hull, Norwich, or Westcliff on Sea. I have become aware, thanks to my many correspondents, that there must be a positive army of Barry Tooks out there somewhere, and I wish them all as I wish myself.

But back to some letters, possibly more revealing than the writers intended.

Of the four thousand letters or so we received during the course of October 1980, I print three. The first is dated 4 October and comes from Sidney Crump of Knowsley, Merseyside.

Dear Mr Took, You and your programme are beginning to irritate me. This is the third letter that I have written to you within the last month. Neither of the previous letters appeared on *Points Of View*, although both were on topical themes, namely the disgusting filth in the French films recently shown on BBC 2, and the goings on in the *Generation Game*. It would appear that the only way to be mentioned on your programme would be to tell you that I have a mother called Gladys, a sister called Ethel, a brother called Percy, a sister-in-law, Nelly, and that I am known as Sid.

Yours in despair,

Sid Crump

PS Noele Gordon didn't ignore me when I wrote to her, so I don't see why you should.

The second is concerned with postscripts and is signed by Ian D. Collins and Philip S. Collins of Sittingbourne, Kent.

Is it the deliberate policy of your programme to read letters which have postscripts such as 'I don't suppose you will read this letter will you', or 'My mum says I have as much chance of this letter being read out as being the next man on the moon', etc.

If this is so, does this mean that if I add one of these infuriating postscripts on the bottom of this letter, I am guaranteed that my letter will be used?

PS my mum bet me a quid that you wouldn't read my letter!

There you are Ian and Philip, happy now?
The third of my October letters (dated 11 October 1980) possibly needs a word of explanation from me. The previous week a correspondent, Lorna Knox of Cambridge, had written saying she'd enjoyed *We The Accused*, and *Mackenzie* and had added rather puzzlingly,

> You, Barry, are jovial and witty and I'm sure your legs are quite lovely.
> PS I dare you to wear shorts next Friday.

So I did and they and my knees were seen for about four seconds. Anyway, the next week I received this letter, which I reproduce in full. It comes from the entire Blackett family of London W.5.

Your programme has been getting pretty silly for some time now and is only watched by our family by accident, i.e. when tuning in early for the 9 o'clock news.

A few weeks ago we were astonished to be confronted by the grisly sight of Mr Took in his knickers, what had led up to this state of affairs must remain a mystery, the mind boggles. But what, we asked ourselves can this possibly have to do with viewers Points of View?

If the gentleman feels compelled to expose himself in this, or any other, way, perhaps the BBC could provide him with a soiled raincoat and drop him off in a suitable alley in the inner suburbs, a location which would seem quite suitable for his doubtful attributes both mental and physical.

Incidently, our family did not share the views relayed with such misty-eyed veneration by Mr Took on the subject of the recent serialized adaptation of "Fair Stood The Wind For France" How a book so full of tension and feeling could be reduced to such a turgid, flacid and not to put too fine a point on it, boring production amazed us. The actors and the scenery looked very pretty indeed . But that was all.

Drama has reached an all time low! We appreciate that budget cuts have to be made, what we cannot understand is why what money there is is used for junk like Angels, Juliet Bravo and the un-utterable MacKenzie. Where are Play For Today? Playhouse? Premiere? Not even a repeat, for weeks! "We, The Accused" was expensively made, but why? The content was'nt worthy of the cost. The "Escape" series was mostly very good, very much up to what we had become used to accepting as BBC standard, but this has been all. Even the repeats from last years bag of single plays were an odd selection, the best of them ignored. What happened to "The Brylcreem Boys"? "In Hiding"? "Story Without A Hero"? "Gentle Folk", "Dreams Of Leaving"? And when is the BBC going to repeat that super trilogy "Matilda's England"?

This letter is a combined view from my family. Our ages run from 18 to 47 and our occupations from housewife to owner/manager of small business.

We are really beginning to feel let down by the BBC.

I'm not going to finish this collection on that rather sour note, but with this from Wendy Sturgess of Kingston upon Thames.

Dear Barry Took, Yet another complaint . . . I am fed up with the recent standard of TV programmes. I used to have two or three box free evenings when I could go to bed early or look at next week's *Radio Times*. But *now* . . .? Well, let's take Nov 9–15. Saturday: Dylan Thomas was riveting. Sunday: magnificent programme on Wild Flowers, followed by such an array of good programmes that there wasn't even time to make a cup of tea. Mon: *Not The Nine O'Clock News* (riotous) plus a fascinating *Horizon* look at horoscopes. Any respite on Tuesday? No, couldn't miss *Man Alive* or *Mountbatten*. Wednesday: tired after a late night but *Strangeways* and *Parkinson* demand to be seen and I wait with bated breath for each new episode of *Mackenzie* on Thursday. Surely Friday will be a washout, but no, we have the Delderfield serial (first class), Playhouse and *Sounds Different*.

Please, Mr Took, can't you persuade the BBC to put on a few more rubbishy programmes so that my overdue library books are returned and my family can wear socks without holes.

I hope you've enjoyed this selection of letters that have been sent to *Points Of View* in the last 18 months. It's only a tiny percentage of our postbag but is, I believe, a fair representation of what our viewers think and feel. My only regret is that there isn't room for more. Well, there is, *just* – the first reproduced in its entirety is as follows, exactly as I received it.

Dear barry took Why Do
you get letters
off people?

The second comes from Diane Simpson, a handwriting analyst, and I reproduce it here because it surprised and delighted me.

> Watching your programme for the first time this evening – I was enchanted to see that the letters you used on the screen were 'genuine' originals rather than a T.V. mock up – supposedly produced to make writing more legible.
>
> Here before my very eyes were your kind, impulsive, revengeful, patient, generous and curious viewer/writers. I can hardly wait for the next programme.

It's the contact with people all over the United Kingdom (and some in Belgium, France, Germany and the Irish Republic) that I find fascinating.

I hope that you, dear reader, have found in this book things to wonder at, disagree with, be irritated by, and also things that have made you smile, and nod your head in agreement. In this country today there are many things that are puzzling, frightening and uncomfortable. What we do have, as I hope that *Points Of View* demonstrates, is that priceless gift – free speech.

Barry Took
St John's Wood.
January 1981

Biography

Barry Took admits that he has been infatuated with show business since childhood. After years of working as a stage hand, a stand up comedian on the music halls, and later appearing in intimate revue in Shaftesbury Avenue, he found the infatuation wearing off somewhat and, in due course, became a radio and TV script writer. His credits include *Round The Horne*, and *Marty* with Marty Feldman, the adaptations of J. B. Morton's *The World Of Beachcomber*, and Stephen Potter's *Oneupmanship*, and the BBC Literacy Project, *On The Move*, *Your Move*, and *Write Away*, which he presented. He is also well known for his frequent appearances on radio where he has chaired many panel games including *Sounds Familiar*, *The Impressionists*, *The News Quiz*, and *Animal, Vegetable and Mineral*. His latest series, *Old Took's Almanac*, has been heard recently on Radio 4. His books include *The Max Miller Blue Book* (based on the music hall act of the legendary Max Miller), and *Laughter In The Air* – a history of radio comedy soon to appear in paperback.

Today he is best known as the presenter of *Points Of View* and *Swap Shop Junior Points of View*. The 'overspill' of letters to these programmes form the basis of this book.